THE WAY OF
BASEBALL

Finding Stillness at 95 MPH

SHAWN GREEN

WITH GORDON McALPINE

Simon & Schuster

New York   London   Toronto   Sydney

Simon & Schuster
1230 Avenue of the Americas
New York, NY 10020

First Simon & Schuster hardcover edition June 2011

SIMON & SCHUSTER and colophon are registered trademarks
of Simon & Schuster, Inc.

For information about special discounts for bulk purchases,
please contact Simon & Schuster Special Sales at
1-866-506-1949 or business@simonandschuster.com.

The Simon & Schuster Speakers Bureau can bring authors
to your live event. For more information or to book an event,
contact the Simon & Schuster Speakers Bureau at
1-866-248-3049 or visit our website at www.simonspeakers.com.

Designed by Akasha Archer

Manufactured in the United States of America

10   9   8   7   6   5   4   3   2   1

Library of Congress Cataloging-in-Publication Data

Green, Shawn.
   The way of baseball : finding stillness at 95 mph / Shawn Green,
Gordon McAlpine.
      p.   cm.
   1. Green, Shawn. 2. Baseball players—United States—Biography.
3. Baseball—Philosophy. I. McAlpine, Gordon. II. Title.
GV865.G67A3 2011
796.357092—dc22
[B]   2010043438

ISBN 978-1-4391-9119-4
ISBN 978-1-4391-9121-7 (ebook)

To Lindsay, Presley, and Chandler:
The three loves of my life

CONTENTS

STILLNESS • 1

SPACE AND SEPARATION • 25

AWARENESS • 47

EGO • 75

PRESENCE • 105

THE ZONE • 129

NONATTACHMENT • 153

GRATITUDE • 175

EPILOGUE • 203

ACKNOWLEDGMENTS • 207

THE WAY OF
BASEBALL

STILLNESS

As I walked from the on-deck circle to the batter's box at Miller Park in the late afternoon of May 23, 2002, I couldn't help but wonder if I was about to get drilled by the next pitch. It was the ninth inning and I had already amassed five hits against the Milwaukee Brewers, including three home runs—in their own ballpark. I wasn't so much worried about the pain of taking a fastball square in the back as I was curious as to how the day would turn out. Being this deep into the zone, I felt more like a spectator than a participant, watching my actions, rather than willing them. I had never had this kind of success in a single game, nor had I ever even seen anyone else achieve such heights, so I wasn't sure what the protocol was.

I dug my back foot into the batter's box and went through my usual routine (I silently debated whether to take a pitch to see where the pitcher, Jose Cabrera, stood in terms of baseball etiquette). As I settled into my stance, I realized

I was still too locked in to burden myself with thinking. I'd simply look for my pitch and swing hard. The first pitch crossed the plate several inches outside; nonetheless, my body felt on time, as I'd felt all day. Ball one. The next pitch was a changeup that I recognized but missed with my fiercest cut. There'd be no backing down this at-bat; I had a once in a lifetime shot at history. The 1-1 pitch was a fastball thigh-high on the inner part of the plate. My timing was perfect and an all-out swing sent my fourth and farthest home run of the day over the fence. Effortless! I was six for six with four home runs and nineteen total bases . . . a Major League record.

Journeying around the bases, I relished the moment: a rare ovation from an opposing crowd and looks of amazement from the infielders as I trotted past. As I approached home plate, I made eye contact with a familiar face in the opposing dugout, Gary Matthews Sr., my former hitting coach. He gave me his characteristic military salute, for which he'd long before earned his nickname, Sarge. For two years in Toronto, he'd worked with me in batting cages across the American League, often four or more hours before game time. Now, Sarge's salute was more than a mere acknowledgment of my record-setting performance. It was recognition for all the work I'd invested over thousands of hours.

As I shook hands with my teammates and acknowledged the standing ovation of the crowd, I reflected on the past. The fruits of my labor here at Miller Park had grown from seeds planted five years earlier, before Sarge had even been hired by my first team, the Blue Jays. In those days, a conflict created a painful rift in my game, my future, my world: a rift that I now understood had created the necessary space for these fruitful seeds to have been planted in the first place, beneath the SkyDome in Toronto.

TORONTO 1997

After two years in the big leagues, I'd already been labeled a slow starter. My hitting seemed to warm with the seasons, heating up in summer, so, along with most of the Blue Jays' faithful, I suspected that '97 would be no different. In May, with springtime almost over, my hitting was indeed still as frigid as the Canadian air, but I wasn't panicked. June was on its way, July after that. Surely I'd find my stroke. This year, however, I faced a new obstacle—being benched—and my opportunities to heat up with the weather were seriously threatened.

Cito Gaston, our manager, had won two World Series and he was much loved by veteran players because of his loyalty to them, as well as his old-school attitudes. Cito viewed many younger players with suspicion. At twenty-four, I'd already accumulated sufficient credentials to be an everyday player (AAA batting title in '94, voted among the top five American League rookies in '95, career average in the mid .280s), but I'd never been given the chance. My rookie year with the Jays I hit .288 with 15 home runs on a last place team, yet I only got to play against right-handed pitchers. By mid-May of '97, Cito finally won out over the front office regarding my playing time. Suddenly, my career prospects were slipping away as I was forced to sit day after day in the dugout watching all the games from the so-called best seat in the house.

After weeks of frustration, I met with general manager Gord Ash and asked him to trade me so I could play somewhere, anywhere. A week or two passed, and every day new trade rumors with my name attached floated around the league until at last Cito had to address it.

It was midafternoon at the Toronto SkyDome, four hours before a night game against the Yankees. I'd put on my uniform and was walking past Cito's open office door when he called, "Hey, Green, come in here and have a seat. I want to talk to you."

My heart thumped as I approached my boss's desk and sat down.

"Look, Shawn, don't think that I don't like you, 'cause I do," Cito said. "I think you have a lot of potential, but . . ." He stopped, considering, maybe searching out a rationale for benching me. "You need to improve your defense. No manager is going to chance it with you the way you play in the field."

I began to squirm in my seat. My first couple of years I'd played scared in right field because, each time I erred, I couldn't help focusing on the irritation on Cito's face. Still, my defense was improving (within two years I'd win the league's Gold Glove Award, though obviously I didn't possess this evidence for the defense at the time).

"Also, Shawn, you need to learn how to pull the ball to hit more home runs because you don't run well enough to steal bases," Cito continued.

"How do you know I can't steal bases if you never give

me the green light to try?" I snapped. "And as for pulling the ball, I know how to turn on the inside pitch."

For a left-handed-batter, *pulling* the ball means connecting with the pitch early and hitting to right field, increasing the chance of a home run. There was nothing I liked more than pulling the ball with power, but I knew that limiting myself to being a dead-pull hitter would reduce my productivity.

Cito wasn't having it. "You can go on your way, Shawn. The meeting's over."

After a few minutes, my heart rate returned to almost normal.

Cito hadn't said anything that had taken me by surprise; still, this was the first time he'd told me point blank what he thought of me as a player. Now it was clear why I was sitting on the bench. I returned to my locker, grabbed my bat, and went to look for Garth Iorg, a minor league coach who was in town temporarily, to ask if he'd throw to me in the batting cage. When I found him he said, "Okay, but make sure you ask Willie."

Willie Upshaw was the hitting coach and he generally marched in lockstep with the boss, Cito. I'd had enough of that regime for now. "I already looked and couldn't find him, so let's just head to the cage," I lied. For the past few weeks, I'd been sneaking into the batting cage without Willie knowing. He was a good guy, but he wasn't helping me become a better hitter.

When I'd started with the Jays in '95, my hitting coach was Larry Hisle. He was a prince of a man who never forgot his own playing days and how hard hitting actually is. He was always encouraging to me. He'd say, "Oh, big man, if I had a swing like yours, I'd still be playing. Just keep working." He stood up for me that year in a coach's meeting, saying, "Why don't we give the kid a chance to play every day, against lefties and righties? He's doing great and we're twenty-five games behind Boston. Let's see what he can do. How can it possibly hurt?" But his advice was ignored and at the end of the season Hisle was replaced by Willie Upshaw.

When Willie arrived in '96, a key component of his job was to convert John Olerud and me into power hitters, which in Willie's eyes meant pulling the ball. Both Willie and Cito had preferred to pull the ball in their playing days, the 1970s and '80s, when being late on a fastball was considered a knock on your manhood. So Oly and I often had to hit under Upshaw's tutelage to work on hooking balls down the right field line.

One afternoon at SkyDome, Cito and Willie instructed Oly and me to stand extremely close to home plate when we were hitting so that every ball would *feel* inside and we'd have to pull the ball. Both of our performances had been subpar the first part of the season. Olerud had won the Major League batting title for the world championship team in '93 and had chased .400 for most of that season. Now, his coaching staff was dictating that he give up twenty to forty points on his stellar batting average in hopes of hitting an extra ten home runs a year. Oly and I talked a lot about how lost we felt at the plate. It's hard enough to get hits even when you're not being forced to change your swing.

So, on that day in May '97, I was anxious to get to the cage with Garth Iorg to get in some extra batting practice without overbearing instruction from Willie or Cito. Besides,

I needed to take out some of the frustrations of my meeting with Cito—I needed to sweat out the pent-up energy.

As Garth and I walked down the clubhouse corridor, which was adorned with photos of the short but sweet Blue Jays' history, we happened to pass an old photo of Willie Upshaw playing first base during his tenure with the Jays. At that moment, the door that led out of the clubhouse and into the undercarriage of the stadium swung open. It was Willie, ten years older than the photo but still in great shape.

There was no avoiding him. "Hey, Willie," I said, "I'm heading to the cage with Garth to take some hacks."

Confused and irritated, he responded with his gravelly baritone, "What's the matter with me?"

"Nothing's the matter with you, but Garth throws right-handed so I want to hit off him."

Willie was not only a lefty, but he threw erratic batting practice.

He replied, "You've got to learn to hit against lefties sometime."

That *really* pissed me off. My three years of platooning against only right-handers was a sore subject with me. I had hit well against lefties in the minor leagues, but had never been given the chance at the Major League level.

I snapped back, "I know how to hit lefties, Willie, but I never get to play against lefties. So, I want to hit off Garth." Meantime, Garth could only awkwardly stand there, anxious for the tension to subside. He was no more comfortable with the confrontation than I was.

Willie's next sentence left me dumbfounded. "No, you can't go to the cage anymore without my supervision."

After a moment of shocked hesitation, I snapped back, "Are you serious?"

He nodded yes.

I stormed off, feeling as if I'd been smacked across the face with my Louisville Slugger. Instead of going to the cage, I headed for the only other place I could take some swings. A shabbily carpeted pathway led from the clubhouse into the dugout, and just off the pathway was a batting tee, a bag of balls, and a net. There, guys would take five to ten swings before they went on-deck, especially in pinch hit situations, because the cage was too far to access during a game.

Now, for me, the tee and tiny net was the only place I could take unsupervised swings.

I grabbed the bag of balls and started hacking away. My swings were 100 percent brute and zero percent finesse. I swung hard not only to release my anger but also to let everyone know how pissed off I was. I didn't say a word but just kept swinging. Many of my teammates and coaches walked past on their way to the dugout to prepare for regular batting practice on the field. Some of them may have already heard about what happened. By watching my furious swings, they knew something was bothering me. My head spun the entire time I was swinging. "How could Willie say that to me? Am I going to get traded? Cito thinks I'm a horrible player!" These thoughts and fears consumed me. I swung and swung until I was dripping sweat, then I grabbed my glove and headed out for the team's four-thirty stretching session.

Out on the field I sat cross-legged, going through the team's stretch routine, worried about my future with the Jays, and that my whole career might be in jeopardy. Though I got along great with my teammates, I knew now that Cito and a handful of others on his coaching staff were just waiting for me to slip up; if I ever got back into the lineup I'd better be on top of my game. The problem was that after my confrontation with Willie I wouldn't be able to step into the batting cage again this whole season—a line had been drawn in the sand. My new challenge was to improve my swing while neither playing in the games nor working in the cage. All I had was the brief, daily team batting practice on the field and the modest little tee in the runway to the clubhouse.

The tee had to work.

Every day thereafter, I'd change into my uniform, grab my bat, and head to the tee and the tiny net. It didn't take long for everyone on the team to know my situation with the coaches. At first, I took my swings at the tee with the same angry and fearful thoughts that had swirled in my head that first day. I was young and prideful, and thus I felt pretty cool for being rebellious for the first time in my life. I can see now that I initiated my tee work merely as a way to get loose and for a chance to parade my ego a little. However, four or five days into it something changed. I began to enjoy it. After the first fifteen or so swings, my mind would quiet and the swings would start to feel more fluid. I began to enjoy the twenty to thirty minutes I spent at the tee every day, even developing a routine of moving the tee to different places in the strike zone. I would visualize game situations and pretend I was facing all of the pitchers that I was currently being forced to merely watch from the distance of my seat in the dugout. I began to notice the sound of the ball *swishing* against the back net, like a perfectly shot basketball. I even made a ritual of placing the ball onto the tee the same way every time. My breathing became rhythmic: inhaling as I put the ball on the tee, holding my breath as I got in my stance, and exhaling as I took my swing. What was happening here? My tee work had started out as a form of punishment, yet suddenly it felt like something else, something more than just a hitting exercise.

Was it becoming a *meditation*?

As a senior at Tustin High School in Southern California, I read *Zen and the Art of Motorcycle Maintenance*, by Robert Pirsig. The book's Eastern perspective struck a resonant chord with me, particularly as I'd come to it wide open to exploring not only the world around me, but also the world within. I devoured other similar books, such as *The Way of the Peaceful Warrior, Zen in the Art of Archery,* and *Siddhartha*. Compelled by the promise of a more enlightened way of living, I continued my informal study of Eastern philosophies during my three years in the minor leagues and my first two seasons in the majors, developing a more meditative approach to the game of life, even as I worked with my coaches to develop a more efficient approach to the game of baseball.

Prior to that fateful day in '97 with Cito and Willie, I'd dabbled in *qigong* meditation. In the winter months, I'd attended a small dojo in Newport Beach, where I learned to control my breathing—in through the nose, out through the mouth—and worked on finding my *qi*, or vital energy, which flows through the body. I loved the calming effect of the work, taking special note of the altered taste in my mouth and the glassy-eyed feeling upon completion of a session. As a novice, I appreciated such physiological feedback to acknowledge my being on the right track. I intended to maintain the work through spring training and into the regular season, but I lost touch with the practice after just a few weeks of baseball and workouts in Florida. (It's not easy dragging yourself out of bed at the crack of dawn to get to the training complex by seven, so setting the alarm for an even earlier hour to facilitate meditation proved no easy task; at the end of a full day of workouts in the hot sun, all I'd want was a quick dinner and the rest and sleep necessary to do it all over again the next day.) It's the most common thing in the world to forfeit a fulfilling routine when one's schedule becomes more demanding. Pouring myself into spring training, I was unaware that meditation could fit unobtrusively into my daily routine, even at the office. Only later in that '97 season, at the batting tee, did my two worlds meld into one.

At first, it seemed accidental that I found my own meditation with a bat in my hand. I know now that there are no accidents—everything is as it's supposed to be. The truth is that my banishment from the batting cage arrived at exactly the right moment. I'd obtained enough apprentice knowledge as a young major leaguer to recognize that my swing was better suited to hit to all fields. Also, I'd read enough books and spent just enough time working on meditation in the off-season to recognize the stillness that arises from transcending the noise of the mind. A couple of dozen sessions into my tee work, I began to notice the same stillness I had touched upon several months prior at the dojo, where

I'd worked on *qigong*. Then, my meditations had been motionless, either seated or standing, whereas now they were centered on movement. I had swung a bat so many times in my life that I really didn't need to think about it. In fact, I was soon to discover that I was better off doing it with no thought at all.

A novice at any skill will fail to find meditation in the practice of that skill until he or she has achieved a level of technical expertise that makes the skill feel like second nature. The pull approach I had been forced to explore with Willie and Cito required my thinking, so it could never have provided the stillness I experienced when I returned to my natural swing.

It took the first couple of weeks of tee work to recover my up-the-middle stroke. But, in my banishment from the cage, I was free to revert to the swing I had been developing since my youth. My priority was to be ready for whatever chance I'd have to return to the lineup. On June 16, the Blue Jays released Ruben Sierra, the former All-Star who had recently been signed as my experimental replacement. My father, Ira, must have blown out some magic candles that day and gotten his birthday wish. The next day, I was back in the lineup for the first time in weeks.

That was the good news.

The bad news was that waiting for me on the pitcher's mound was Greg Maddux, one of the best of all time. I'd find out soon enough if my solitary hours spent at the tee would pull me through.

I stepped to the plate in the second inning for my first at-bat against Maddux more composed and calm than I'd expected to be. I drove a 1-1 changeup over the fence in right-center field for a home run. Not only was the pitch of the off-speed variety that historically had given me trouble, but it had come out of the hand of a man destined for the Hall of Fame largely because of the effectiveness of that specific pitch. I followed up that first at-bat with another hit in the fifth inning, then a second home run in the eighth inning. Thereafter, I became an everyday player and raised my batting average about sixty points in a month's time.

I had a new best friend—the batting tee.

For the first month after I re-entered the starting lineup, my tee routine remained very basic. I'd place the baseball on the tee with the four seams perpendicular to me, take a breath, and swing with my best up-the-middle stroke. I'd then take another breath, and repeat the process, over and over. Next, I would move the tee around to work on hitting pitches in different locations. The process was similar to what I'd done in the cage my dad built in the backyard of our house when I was a kid. The difference now was that I was not thinking about mechanics; I was focusing only on my breathing and on the ball.

The improvement in my swing and my newfound comfort at the plate got me hooked on the tee work. Being a spiritual seeker was a passion, but during the baseball season, hitting came first. It was my livelihood. Up to this point, these two worlds had not yet fully entwined. The meditative and subliminal effects of the tee work were more subtle than the immediate improvement at the plate. Inner stillness grew slowly, like the roots of a fruit tree spreading under the soil. However, as I continued my work throughout that summer of '97, these aspects gradually became apparent and eventually as important to me as my batting success. I began to thirst for those twenty-minute sessions each day at the tee, not just as a means to achieving more at the plate, but as a way into peace and stillness.

In time, the tee itself became an object worthy of contemplation. . . .

Initially, I made do with whatever brand of tee the grounds crew set up at the net. Most stadiums had the awkward, yellow Atec brand tee, which was made of hard rubber that had a plastic feel. The tee could be moved up and down only from thigh high to midstomach and every time I took a swing, I'd feel my bat striking more of the tee than the ball. Worse, the thing tipped over on impact. Some stadiums had similar tees made by Louisville Slugger or Franklin that were slightly better, but still didn't provide a natural feel.

Then, late that summer, our team equipment manager Jeff Ross showed me a new tee he had bought from Joe Tanner, a scout from Bradenton, Florida. The base was a small, square piece of wood about half an inch thick. The vertical piece was a telescoping stem that screwed into the base and had a soft but durable rubber cradle to hold the ball. Easily unscrewed into two pieces for transport, one could raise and lower the tee to work on extreme high and low pitches; also, the rubber cradle was so pliable that upon contact it didn't even feel like the ball was set on a tee.

I was in love.

I never envisioned becoming a connoisseur of batting tees, but the tool had become the crux of my two worlds: baseball and spirituality. I put a felt pen to the base of the

Tanner Tee and branded it with a big 15, my number. For the last two months of that season and the remaining ten years of my career, a Tanner Tee travelled with me on every road trip.

I'd begin my work with the Tanner Tee at its maximum height, swinging with a chopping motion, as if I were felling a tree. After several swings, I'd lower the tee a little, taking as many swings as was necessary to capture the same motion of chopping wood at the new height. This continued until the ball was as low as the tee would allow, just below my knees. By starting at the highest point and working down, I ingrained in my swing a chopping feel, thus guarding against long, loopy upward swings. Also, the height of the ball tended to mirror the depth of my meditative state. By the time the ball was at my knees, I'd be deep into the flow of my practice. Sometimes, it was difficult to get to that magical place. On those days, I'd take more swings at the top of the zone. Other times, the process moved rapidly. There was no clock, no race. The process unfolded on its own.

Sure, friends on the team would razz me about my solitary work. Ed Sprague poked fun at me by mimicking some of my unorthodox drills. He was a right-handed hitter, but he'd playfully mock me by standing at the tee in my left-handed stance and overexaggerate my drills. Other teammates found it peculiar that I packed my own tee in my bag for every road trip. Someone was always commenting, "Don't forget your tee!" It was all in fun and always good for a laugh (back-and-forth banter is part of life in the big leagues). However, as my success on the field continued, the joking sessions gradually turned into interrogation sessions as teammates and opposing players took serious notice of my work in the cage. Smart hitters, like Ed Sprague, gained respect for my theories on hitting. Many of the drills in my practice evolved from discussions or observations of other hitters around baseball. We all share with each other all the time.

As stillness entered my life, my relationship with the ever-challenging external world also began to change. Late in the '97 season, I noticed that the outer world wasn't affecting my inner world to the degree that it once had. A negative newspaper article or comment on the street still might cause me a momentary burst of anger or irritation, but the emotions weren't as charged as they were before. More important, the negativity didn't linger obsessively in my head for hours or whole days. Soon, I stopped reading the newspapers altogether, after good games as well as bad. Whatever was said about me, positive or negative, did not have to affect the way I felt about myself.

Of course, thoughts and concerns still inhabited my mind. Such is the nature of human existence. But now the daily practice of stillness altered my relationship to those thoughts, aiding me to control them rather than the other way around. Finding stillness strengthened my ability to recognize and disarm menacing thoughts, thereby helping me maintain my own sense of being. Just as I changed my relationship with the baseball by stopping it and placing it on the tee, meditation enabled me to change my relationship with my thoughts.

In the cage, I would place a baseball on the tee, take a breath, stroke the ball to the back of the net, and then repeat the process, over and over. Outside the cage, I was now able to do something similar with my mind. A stressful or agitating thought would come into my head, so I would take a breath, then calmly stroke that thought away, leaving behind only stillness.

Contrary to general misconceptions, meditation is not about training oneself to live without thought; rather, it's about training oneself to move beyond one's thoughts. Skilled practitioners may find themselves experiencing brief moments of no-mind, though not even the most enlightened among them remain in that state at all times. The chatter of the mind always returns. However, the more one practices meditation, the more one can control the mind and in so doing, expend less energy *reacting* to the endlessly challenging circumstances of our lives. Upon lifting the heaviness of charged thoughts, one's life becomes much lighter.

One example of such a significant shift in my perspective occurred at a game in Seattle in mid-September of '97. It was four months since the conflict that launched my unexpected spiritual journey, and I was not only improving my performance at the plate, but also my relationship with the fans. I'd always been conscientious about signing autographs, but I had regarded most interactions with the public as something of a chore. I was too wrapped up in my own thoughts to connect with the people in the stands and so sensitive to criticism of my performance that I'd built a protective wall to keep safe from it. How could I have been anything but distant? However, after several months of working in a place of stillness to become less susceptible to the opinions of others, I allowed the wall between myself and the fans to come down.

We were finishing batting practice as a sellout crowd made its way into Seattle's Kingdome to see their first place Mariners, which featured All-Stars Ken Griffey, Jr., Alex Rodriguez, Randy Johnson, and Jay Buhner. I was shagging fly balls in right field when a kid with a baseball glove near the foul pole asked me to toss him a ball. No longer stressed out about preparing for the game, as I would have been in the past, I realized I could provide the kid with a memorable moment at the ballpark. Besides, it seemed like it'd be fun to play catch with him. I threw him the ball and indicated for him to throw it back; at first, he seemed worried about keeping the ball, but after I assured him it would be his when our game of catch was over, he threw the ball back. After we tossed it back and forth a couple of times, an unexpected thing happened. Another kid held his glove up for me to throw it to him. So I did (after again reassuring the first kid that he'd get the ball at the end). Before I knew it I was throwing this one ball to kid after kid after kid, my only criteria being that each needed to have a baseball glove. Before long, batting practice was over and I was left by myself in the outfield with an entire stadium of kids holding up their gloves and yelling for me to throw them the ball. I couldn't believe that no one tried to steal the ball (I guess the people in the Pacific Northwest are exceptionally honest). This went on for forty-five minutes.

I thought I was providing a memorable ballpark moment to someone else.

Yet I'm the one who'll never forget it.

That night, I felt a connection with an entire stadium of people. In the past, I'd have been too caught up in nervous preparation for the game I was about to play to experience such a thing, but now I knew that my tee work had seen to my preparation. No longer a slave to worry, about either the upcoming game or what my coaches and teammates might think of my antics, I was truly free to enjoy a spontaneous moment. Later, I would try to recreate it in other stadiums, but beautiful moments cannot always be planned. (Besides, whenever I tried it in New York or Boston it was never long before somebody would just make off with the "souvenir.") Because I had the stillness of mind to enjoy what the world was offering me, I was able to connect with others in a new way. As the clock hit six-forty, I tossed the ball back to the original kid, waved to the crowd, and headed toward the clubhouse to switch jerseys in time to make it back onto the field for the game. As I ran off, the entire stadium gave me a loud ovation, which felt much more affectionate than any performance-induced cheering. My teammates razzed me a little, but that didn't bother me. I'd had fun with forty-some-odd thousand fans.

The next day, Blue Jays announcer Buck Martinez told me that in all the years he'd been in baseball that was the "coolest thing [he] had ever seen." He'd recognized a shift in me and, though he didn't know about my work at the tee every day beneath the stadium, his kind words were further evidence that I was progressing in the right direction.

The '97 season ended on a high note. I finished what was potentially going to be a career-damaging year so strongly that I solidified myself into an everyday player, and the team rewarded me with a nice two-year contract (more than the boost to my bank account, the raise signified a new level of commitment from the team). In addition, Cito and the faction of coaches that had been less than supportive during that first phase of my career were all let go at the end of the season. I felt as if the shackles had been removed and that I was about to enter my true rookie season come '98, even though I already had more than three years in the Major Leagues under my belt.

My measurable growth as a player was obvious from a statistical perspective, but my internal growth was equally important to me. Of course, unlike hitting, spiritual growth can't be quantified. But I didn't need measurements. The ball sat still, and I hit it, period. My mantra wasn't a candle flame or a chant, as in some forms of meditation. My mantra was the ball motionless; the only movement I focused on was the movement of my breath. The swing occurred on its own. Absorbed in the action of hitting, I felt my body moving, I saw only the ball, and I heard the contact of the wood on the ball followed by the swishing sound of the ball hitting the back of the cage—a beautiful practice.

I had reduced hitting, an extremely difficult activity, to its most basic form. As a result, I took each swing with full attention.

Previously, when a pitcher threw a ball to me, the ball was in control. I reacted to the ball's speed and movement. Since the pitcher was the one who threw the ball, I also reacted to the pitcher. Of course, in my tee routine I no longer worked against the pitcher and the ball. Now, there was no pitcher, and the ball was simply sitting there waiting for me to hit it. I didn't need to speed up or slow down to time a moving pitch. Instead, I could take the same rhythmic swing over and over, reinforcing quality habits until they became second nature. In essence, I reversed my relationship with the baseball.

And on a deeper level, I was learning to step out of time.

When baseball players talk about hitting, they often talk about time. In sports pages across the country, you'll find articles in which a player says, ". . . my *timing* is off," or ". . . I found my *timing* at the plate," or ". . . I'm looking for my *timing*." I too worked continually to find and maintain my timing in games. But I learned that the most efficient way to accomplish this was to remove myself each day to a place of stillness, a place removed from time.

There, in that twenty-minute bubble, I'd connect my swing to my deepest sense of being, training myself to become less reactive and more in control both at the plate and in life. Afterward, I could re-enter the world of time as a more centered and emotionally quiet person (as well as a better-prepared hitter).

Prior to my meditative practice taking root, I lived my off the field life in much the same manner that I approached hitting: reactive. I might show up to the stadium fuming over a critical article in the local paper, distracted and intent on proving something. Hitting a Major League curve ball is hard enough without attaching to it a personal agenda. And the potential distractions of being a public figure are not limited to how one responds to press coverage. The same holds true for walking across the street.

In those early years, when Blue Jays fans stopped me to say, "Wow! Shawn Green! You're my favorite!" it filled me with pride; however, when those same fans tossed off critical comments, such as "Hey, what happened last night on that ball you dropped?" I was left obsessing over an error that I had already lost sleep over the night before. Finding stillness, however, enabled me to understand the pitfalls of allowing the ever-changing external world to dictate my inner world. If one stranger's opinion could actually change my stress level, anger level, and overall well-being, then who was actually at the controls of my life? And yet that is how most of us live, whether we're in the public eye or not.

Ultimately, hitting off the tee provided me a much needed refuge of deepening absorption and stillness. The practice changed with time and I got more adept at creating drills that finely tuned my swing. The routine I did in '97 was more basic than the one I was doing by '98, which, in turn, was a stepping stone to my practice in '99 and beyond. Initially, teammates and coaches considered my drills more than a little unorthodox. But, like many other businesses, baseball tolerates the unconventional so long as you're getting hits. Now, it feels good to think I may have had an influence on the game that extended beyond the stats on the back of my baseball card. Over the last six or seven years of my career, I no longer needed to bring a Tanner Tee with me to opposing stadiums, because by then every cage in the big leagues had at least one or two sitting inside. Of course, I still brought my own tee (the little things matter the most), but I couldn't help smiling at the sight of all the other Tanner Tees, at the big league proliferation of that old scout from Bradenton's homemade work.

• • •

For a major-league hitter, nothing seems more menial than working off a batting tee, but it's actually in menial tasks that we find the best opportunities to practice stillness. I never outgrew my practice at the tee. Rather, I continued to discover other so-called menial tasks that also could serve as practices of stillness. Exercising is a great domain for meditation. Lifting weights, I concentrate on my breathing while at the same time feeling the subtle movements of my body. I learned from my yoga instructor, Steve Rogers, that "all of your movements are anchored in the breath." In weightlifting, moving from one repetition to the next requires an inhalation and an exhalation. The weight comes down . . . breathe in; the weight goes up . . . breathe out.

As a professional athlete, such repetitive physical workouts offered many opportunities to seek stillness. But if physical activity or sitting meditation doesn't fit into your daily schedule, you can still find stillness by focusing in a new way on your daily tasks, specifically, on the "mindless," menial ones.

Instead of washing dishes or mowing the lawn in a distracted state, why not do it with full attention? By using your own breath to anchor you to stillness, you can connect with the present moment. For example, in my tee work I'd place the ball on the tee and take a breath, step back and take a breath, swing the bat, hit the ball and take a breath, bend and pick up another ball and take a breath, place the new ball on the tee and take another breath. Ultimately, the mindful breathing, which served to focus my attention, was as much a part of the exercise as the actual swinging of the bat.

Concentrate on whatever you're doing.

Life is full of menial tasks, which means it is full of

SPACE AND SEPARATION

Finding stillness through my tee work proved a life-altering discovery. The practice was simple: focus on my breathing, feel the swing without thinking about it, and hit line drives up the middle. My practice swings made their way into games and, by the end of the '97 season, I'd found my tool for transformation, both on a spiritual and physical level. Additionally, the tee work provided me a safe place from which to explore new possibilities as a hitter, which I engaged during the off-season months between '97 and '98 when I confronted negative tendencies in my swing—imperfect stride, hand position, and shoulder rotation—that dated all the way back to my Little League days.

First, my stride had always been on the longer side, in regards to both space and time. Ideally, a hitter wants a short stride, so his swing can be quicker, providing extra milliseconds to judge the pitch. Ted Williams often said that swinging at better pitches is the key to getting more hits. The catch, however, is that it is usually that extra length of the swing that provides power. My former teammate Paul Molitor had *no* stride. He just picked up his front heel and put it back down. This made his swing extremely efficient and contributed to his amassing more than three thousand hits in a Hall of Fame career, but he didn't hit many home runs. On the other hand, Reggie Jackson had a big stride and big swing, striking out often but hitting more than five hundred homers in *his* Hall of Fame career. Only the very best all-around hitters in each generation, guys like Barry Bonds and Albert Pujols, have the ability to take short, quick strides and still have home run power. I could never do that. The goal for me was to find a happy medium.

Complicating the problem was that I tended to step toward home plate rather than toward the pitcher, which is known as *diving in*. Instinctively, I was better able to read the pitch by moving my head and eyes toward the plate; however, this misdirection brought every pitch closer than necessary to my body, which made it harder for me to put the barrel of the bat on the ball because I lacked the space to get to inside strikes. Meantime, pitches over the middle felt as if they were on the inside corner, meaning the only pitch I could hit truly well was the one on the outside part of the plate. And Major League pitchers very quickly get stingy with putting pitches in the location you prefer.

My other two unhealthy tendencies were both related to the loading of my upper body for an aggressive swing. Most hitters push their hands and bat back as they stride for the ensuing swing. An analogy is the act of throwing a punch. The first move is to cock one's arm back before thrusting the fist forward to create the blow. The farther back the fist is loaded, the more power in the punch. However, the farther back the loading, the longer the time the punch takes to be delivered. As a hitter, I brought my hands back as far as they would go, to the extent that my right arm was no longer bent. In hitting, this is referred to as *barring out* the front arm. Additionally, I rotated my right shoulder too far toward home plate in an attempt to generate more bat speed by coiling backward. I'd developed these habits of overextension as a child, simply by trying to hit the baseball harder. Unfortunately, they'd accompanied me all the way to the big leagues.

Such imperfections might make you wonder how I ever got a hit at all! However, the truth is that all hitters have negative tendencies in their swings; the challenge is to navigate through obstacles and work with what you have. I probably could have played an entire career simply putting bandages on these issues by finding strictly physical ways to compensate. However, I'd never have developed the power and production that I found after that '97 season.

Through my tee work, I obtained the necessary mental space to finally solve problems like a stride being too long or a right shoulder being overrotated toward home plate. In the process, I began to answer for myself the question of just how good I might be at this game and how problems of all sorts might be overcome. No longer content to merely patch up weak spots, I was beginning to form a vision of how to heal them.

What of all the work I'd put in on the diamond since the time I was a child first in love with baseball? Was it wasted?

No, it was all a part of the process.

I'd just never arrived at a proper solution to the problems with my swing because my mind had always been filled with analytical thoughts. Those four summer months in '97 of swinging in stillness created the necessary space and emptiness of mind for the solution to just come to me. (We often solve life's most complicated dilemmas when we sleep on it, or in my case meditate on it.)

I began to see my three swing issues in a new light that off-season. One day, it hit me. I had always viewed the challenges in my swing as three separate issues and had tried to fix each problem on an individual basis. In reality, all three issues were the result of *one* underlying flaw in my swing: the upper half of my body and the lower half of my body were working as *one connected piece.* In other words, my hands going back too far during my stride, ultimately causing my arm to bar out, was directly proportional to my stride being too long. During the time that my foot was in the air, my arms and bat *had* to go further back in the other direction to act as a counterbalance. The tendency for my stride to dive in toward the plate also forced my right shoulder to turn in toward the plate with it, and vice versa.

To fix these problems, I had to begin with my setup.

Through the '97 season, I'd always had a *square stance*. In other words, my back foot and front foot were in a straight line, parallel to home plate and in line with the pitcher. The other two stance options are a *closed stance*, wherein the front foot is closer to home plate than the back foot, aiming more of the back toward the pitcher, or an *open stance*, wherein the front foot is further from the plate than the back foot, aiming more of the stomach toward the pitcher. In my square stance, my right foot, right hip, and right shoulder were all perfectly aligned, aiming at the pitcher. However, as I took my stride I'd wind up aiming more toward the shortstop than the pitcher, with my right shoulder aimed somewhere between the third baseman and the shortstop. Thus, my up-the-middle approach was defeated when I actually took my swing. How to correct the problem? Instead of *fighting* where my body wanted to go, I went with it. Keeping my entire body locked into its natural position, I danced my feet around clockwise so that, when I swung, my right shoulder would be aimed directly at the pitcher rather than at the hole between third base and shortstop. I looked down and saw that I was now in an open stance with my feet, but my shoulder was in perfect alignment for hitting up the middle. The open stance that I practiced for the rest of my career was born.

My next step was to get into that open stance and work through my natural tendency to bar out my right arm. I pushed my arms back as far as they could go, enabling me to shorten my swing, since I wouldn't have to load up as I took my stride. However, I noticed that the farther I pushed my hands back, the farther my right shoulder turned in toward the shortstop. I wanted to keep that shoulder straight. But that's when I had my big discovery. If I pushed my arms back, while at the same time I opened up my right hip in the opposite direction, I could prevent that right shoulder from turning in! This proved to be the key to resolving my swing issues. At the midpoint of my body, my hips separated my swing into two pieces, the upper half and the lower half. Previously, my right shoulder, right hip, and right ankle were all perfectly aligned and moved as one piece. Now, I had found a way to sever that connection and enable my differ-ent body parts to work independently, thus making my swing much more efficient. My right hip and right knee formed my control mechanism. From that day forward, anytime I felt my shoulder turning in too much or my hands moving too far back, I simply pushed my hip and knee slightly clockwise to lock my upper body back into place.

My initial reasons for making these changes were to free up the inside part of the plate and to shore up my weaknesses as a hitter, but in the process I had unwittingly created much more power in my swing. It stands to reason. The lower half of my body was now twisted toward the second baseman while my upper body was facing the pitcher, thereby creating more torque as my body unwound with each swing. Visualize a toy airplane with a propeller and a rubber band. The more you rotate that propeller, the more tension is placed on the rubber band. The greater the tension, the faster the propeller will spin upon release—simple physics.

I still had one remaining swing issue to work through: the stride.

It was one thing to create the proper setup and stance, but it was a greater challenge to maintain the integrity of my positioning as I took my stride. Nonetheless, I knew that if I succumbed to my old habit of striding in toward home plate, I'd undermine all the body separation that my new positioning sought to create. My front foot still wanted to dive in; after all, it was now positioned farther than ever from home plate. But, in my stillness at the tee, I found an answer to the nagging call of habit. Using white athletic tape, I put a line on the floor of the batting cage, providing a border across which I did not allow myself to stride. With each swing I looked down to make sure I hadn't crossed the line. Mechanics alone were insufficient to overcome the old habit, however. I knew that I also needed to create a mental image of the proper stride that I could focus on each time I swung (taking care never to slide back into thinking my way through each swing). So I called upon my imagination to control my stride, and it answered my call.

I discovered that I could actually imagine with my foot and my shoulder.

I imagined with my front foot that I was striding to hit a pitch that was way inside and in the process managed to avoid diving in toward home plate; a mere fraction of a second later, I imagined with my front shoulder that I was going after a pitch that was on the outside corner. My lower body moved on an inside pitch, my upper body on an outside pitch. Thus, separation! The success of these two almost simultaneous intentions ultimately awakened my awareness into my right hip and torso area as a feeling of torque and potential energy arose there that I had never before felt as a hitter.

To most people, imagining with my foot and with my shoulder probably sounds insane. It surely would have sounded that way to me prior to practicing my meditation that summer. The only way to imagine with my foot was to place all my awareness there. And the only way to place all my awareness in my foot was to remove that awareness from my head.

Prior to this work, I had never considered that awareness could reside some place other than the head. How would I have known? After all, most of us go about our whole lives with our awareness trapped in the mind. We believe we *are* our thoughts and egos and nothing more. I always suspected there was more to my true essence than my incessant and repetitive thoughts and the insatiable desires of my ego. I had been searching for that greater part of me via the exploration of Zen and meditation, but it wasn't until that meditative work took root in my swing that I truly began to disconnect from my thoughts and connect with my deeper sense of being.

I used to believe that the goal of meditation was to *stop* thoughts. But, as I did my work off the tee, I learned that my concept of meditation was inaccurate (maybe highly enlightened people are able to stop their thoughts after years of practice, but that wasn't realistic for me). Rather than stopping thoughts, meditation is about shifting one's awareness *out* of thought by focusing attention on something else.

The tool for accomplishing this feat is often a *mantra*, or point of focus. Each time your awareness falls back into the mind's snare, you shift your attention back to the candle flame, the chant, or whatever mantra you employ. Imagine someone meditating with her mantra being a series of words she repeats over and over. As her mind starts to wander off into thoughts, she reconnects her attention to her mantra, and thus separates from those thoughts. At the tee, the flow of the routine became my mantra: take a breath, focus on the ball, swing, take a breath, place a new ball on the tee, then repeat. The work consisted of my swinging in a place of no thought, learning to peel my awareness away from my mind and redirect it into my body. Soon, I was able to move my attention out of my head and into body parts (my foot, my shoulder), shifting my awareness from one to the next without encumbering the movement, or flow, with any thought.

It took me a few weeks of focusing on my new swing intentions to get the mechanics ingrained. Once ingrained, I had a new approach that became second nature. My tee work returned to the deeper, daily meditation that I had created the summer before, except now my swing was much improved; my body parts were no longer pulling each other into unwanted directions, my stance was open and my body torqued, my stride moved straight toward the pitcher and when my front foot landed the coiled position I had created in my stance remained intact.

I worked daily on my new swing through the holidays and into spring training of 1998. My new manager, Tim Johnson, and hitting coach, Gary Matthews Sr., aka Sarge, viewed me as an integral cog of the offense. I was slated to bat third in the lineup, and I didn't want to disappoint. During the off-season, my work had been done only in the cage, and so I was anxious to discover how my new approach would work in the real world.

Taking my new swing onto the field for team batting practice was like having a new toy. As spring training passed and the season began, balls came off my bat with a new, loud, *crack!* akin to the likes of my power-hitting teammates Carlos Delgado and Jose Canseco. Each week, I launched more and more moon shots during batting practice, farther and farther into the bleachers. I was now playing every day and hitting in the top of the lineup and for the first time in my career I had a bit of a swagger. I enjoyed talking smack to Carlos and Jose during batting practice as I launched balls into the deep parts of the bleachers that previously only they had reached. There I was, the skinny line-drive hitter hanging with the big boys—and I loved it. Soon, my approach to our daily team batting practice transformed. My new attitude as a power hitter collided with the gamesmanship that Carlos and I had always indulged in the clubhouse to change the way I took batting practice, introducing a childlike playfulness that in conjunction with my tee work would soon transform my career.

Carlos was my teammate for nearly ten of my sixteen years in professional baseball. He was by my side for my first eight years as a pro (including three years in the minor leagues). Highly intelligent both on and off the field, he was always the teammate I admired most; I came to feel about him almost as if he were an older brother. In the minor leagues, Carlos put up numbers I never thought I could match: 30 home runs and 100 plus RBIs. Even in our first couple of years together in the Major Leagues, I still didn't imagine myself capable of such production. Carlos was a powerful, grown man, whereas I was just a lanky kid. I had always strived to be a .300 hitter with respectable power— inclined to emulate a player like John Olerud, who was built like me and had the same line-drive approach—so Carlos' ability to hit the long ball was never a source of envy. I'd never felt competitive toward him in baseball; sure, he and I always loved to compete when it came to playing cards in the clubhouse. However, one day in Toronto in early June '98, the smack talk moved from the card table to our team batting practice.

My game was about to change.

We usually took BP in groups of four; each group got fifteen minutes to take as many swings as they could. The other players shagged balls on the field and tended to their individual work until it was their group's turn to hit. This was the first year Carlos and I had been in the same hitting group on a daily basis. He was the cleanup hitter and I was number two in the lineup (with right-handed Jose Canseco hitting third between us lefties). Coaches take care of the guys who have the greatest burden of producing runs, so we were given first choice as to which coach we wanted to hit during BP. Carlos and I preferred Jim Lett.

There's always bantering amongst hitters as to who's going to hit the farthest home run, get the most hits in a row, and so on. Carlos began his round of six swings, and I taunted him, "I bet you can't hit a ball off Windows," which was the stadium's glass-fronted restaurant, from which the tables looked onto the field from high above the centerfield wall.

Three swings in, we all heard a pure *crack!*

The ball left Carlos' bat, towering toward centerfield, and ricocheted hard off the bulletproof glass.

He strutted out of the cage with a wide grin. "That's how the big boys do it! But you don't worry about the long ball, Greenie, just keep getting on base. I'll be sure to drive you in."

Sarge watched the whole thing. He chuckled from where he hung on the back of the net that surrounded the hitting area. "Are you going to let him talk to you like that, Greenie? Show him how it's done." He was always quick to stir the pot.

I took six of my hardest cuts, aiming at the restaurant in centerfield. On my last swing I hit my best bolt, which cleared the fence in centerfield. Still, it was short of the restaurant. I walked out of the cage feeling happy about my effort, but Carlos deflated me as he laughed, "Little man hit it!"

Heading into the clubhouse to prepare for that night's game, I turned to Carlos and said, "I'll bet in BP I can hit more home runs to centerfield than you can."

"Centerfield?" he asked.

It's easier to hit home runs down the line than to centerfield; most big league centerfield walls are roughly 400 feet away, whereas down the lines the fences are only about 330 feet away. I knew better than to challenge Carlos to a straight-up home run derby because I knew the dangerous temptation of gearing my swing to pull the ball down the line. (Hadn't my issues with Cito and Willie been about avoiding that very thing?) My recent work in the cage, which was geared to improve my up-the-middle approach but in the process was increasing my power to all fields, suggested that swinging harder wouldn't damage my swing so long as I remained focused on hitting the ball to centerfield. I trusted my daily tee work to keep my swing disciplined.

"That's right, centerfield," I said.

The next day, Carlos, Sarge, and I set the parameters for our game as we got loose before our group's fifteen-minute BP session. A sign on the right-centerfield wall of the Sky-Dome would serve as the foul pole. Anything hit to the right of the sign would be foul, ensuring we wouldn't try to pull the ball. Next, we set up a scoring system: one point for a ball hit over the wall, two points into the seats, three points into the second deck of the stadium, and four points off Windows. Sarge would serve as umpire. Finally, we set the stakes: At the end of every month, the loser had to buy dinner for both the winner and Sarge at the restaurant of their choice. At every stadium we subsequently visited, the foul pole and point system would have to be reset because ballpark configurations were different. And, in this way, our batting practice home run derby was born.

It was fun. More than that, this simple contest had an enormous impact on my career. Initially, Carlos and I intended only to add flavor and intensity to a long season by bringing light-hearted competition into our daily routines. I had always heard coaches admonish players to "practice how they want to play." Though I wasn't a big home run hitter at that early stage of my career, I began to wonder what would happen if I practiced hitting home runs every day to parts of the field that weren't optimal for hitting home runs. Dead center—the biggest part of the ballpark . . . Coaches had always wanted me to hit for more power, but, oddly, they'd never told me to *practice* hitting home runs during batting practice. Instead, they'd give mechanical suggestions as to what changes in my swing or approach would help me hit more home runs, but they never suggested I simply practice hitting the ball as far as I could.

Often, the simplest ideas are the best.

Because of the framework of our friendly competition, I needed to swing all out, every time. I couldn't beat Carlos by hitting balls that barely cleared the wall. Rather than use the same easy swing I practiced at the tee, I swung with 100 percent of the force my body could muster, actually swinging harder during BP than in the real games! We had about thirty swings each and, by the time we finished, both Carlos and I would be dripping with sweat. After a couple of months of his whipping me on a regular basis (during which I paid for dinners at two of the best restaurants in North America), I began to hold my own. Hits that used to barely make it over the fence in centerfield began to make it to the seats. Balls I hit to the opposite field began landing where right-handed power hitters drove homers to their stronger side, their pull side. Eventually, I was hitting balls off of Windows, and a handful of times I actually hit balls over the glass and into the open-air section of the restaurant located just below the Jumbotron.

During my tee work, my swings remained smooth and easy, each taken at a 50 to 70 percent effort. Desired mechanics were repeated in a place of stillness and thus ingrained, regardless of the force of the swings. However, the ball was always stationary on the tee, whereas movement and pace are essential elements of hitting. BP became my vehicle for crafting the timing of my stride with the moving pitch, bringing my tee work into the real world. After mechanics are in place, the biggest challenge a hitter faces is timing his swing with the moving ball; inversely, the art of pitching is all about disrupting that timing. For example, Pedro Martinez was untouchable in the late '90s not because he threw harder than anyone else but because both his fastballs and off-speed pitches looked the same coming out of his hand. Such deception, along with great control and movement, makes it tough for a hitter to get the barrel of the bat on the ball.

The BP game, which provided me a way to practice maintaining separation and stillness in a dynamic environment where timing was critical, became the bridge between my tee work and the real games, between my meditation and the real world. After all, there was little point in my having a great swing while working off the tee if it was to fall apart as soon as the ball was moving toward me.

Could a skinny kid who'd come up hitting line drives actually become a power hitter in the big leagues?

As the '98 season progressed and I grew more adept, I noticed a subtle nuance in the middle of my swing—a slight pause between the completion of my stride and the forward movement of the bat. What I discovered was the emergence of *space*. I hadn't noticed this space in my tee work because the pause was so subtle: the easier the swing, the less separation, the smaller that space. With my vicious swings during BP, however, I discovered that the space existed at a midpoint between the coiling of my body and the unraveling of that position. It is similar to the movement of breathing. There is a slight pause between an inhalation and an exhalation. The deeper the breath, the more pronounced the space. It's impossible to switch from an inhalation to an exhalation without some sort of pause, no matter how brief that pause may be.

All the power in my swing arose out of that empty space. The stride and the body separation were necessary steps, but the space itself was where my job ended and the forces of nature took over. Though lasting only a fraction of a second, the space sometimes felt like an eternity, making a ninety-five miles per hour fastball seem to float in like a beach ball. If I liked the pitch, my swing would begin with my lower half, legs and hips, rotating forward while my upper body stayed back. Next, the turning legs and hips would sling my upper body and bat forward with tremendous force. At that point, I wasn't swinging; something was swinging me. To illustrate this further, consider again your breathing; sometimes it's difficult to differentiate whether you're breathing or whether the world is breathing you. Ninety-nine percent of the time, we pay no attention to breathing, but it still happens.

In the past, whenever my bat felt slow, which inevitably happens in a 162-game schedule, I concentrated on speeding up my hands. Like most hitters, I thought I was supposed to swing a bat with my arms. After discovering separation and space, I realized that the best way to hit was to not swing at all, but to get the body in the proper, separated position, then simply allow the body to naturally uncoil. The bat then falls into the perfect slot and comes through effortlessly with great velocity. It sounds simple, but there is a catch. The stride and all the body movements leading up to the swing must be fluid and happen right on time. That's the tricky part, the timing, which differentiates mediocre stretches from hot streaks. If the stride is late, then the bat rushes forward, thereby forfeiting the swing's separation and space. If the stride is early, then the torqued position of the body becomes tense and less effective. For the optimal swing, the striding foot has to land at an instant I came to think of as "the last possible part of early."

When it comes to such subtlety, awareness is imperative.

For most of us, our awareness becomes trapped within our heads. We are so lost in the fantasies of our minds—egoistic images of who we *think* we are or *should* be—that we fail to truly experience the world around us. Instead, we merely *think* the world. Meditation, practiced in any effective format, trains us to exist and function *apart* from the mind and ego, allowing us to experience the present moment. In my meditative practice at the tee, my awareness attached itself to my body and its movements. In those twenty-minute sessions, I was no longer thinking through my swings; rather, I merely watched as the swings happened. Whenever self-consciousness crept into my head, I'd shift that awareness back into my striding foot, my shoulder, or my breathing. On many days, I moved beyond even my connection to the body and felt I had actually *become* the act of hitting, so absorbed in what I was doing that I lost my sense of self.

Through this daily work, I created a kind of bubble around what I came to recognize as my true essence. All that I previously had thought I was (mind, ego, and emotions), was pushed to the surface of that bubble, away from my true essence, which floated at the center. And what filled the gap that separated this essence from the surface of that bubble? Emptiness. Space. Just as hitting a baseball became effortless when separation and space characterized my swing, overcoming life's daily stresses became effortless when I moved space into everyday situations and conflicts. For example, if someone cut me off on the freeway I'd separate from my rising anger and *watch* the heat and tension rising in my body; in this process, I gained separation from my highly charged emotions and thereby diffused them.

Author Eckhart Tolle teaches that a simple way to experience separation and space is to pay attention to your emotions when watching an intense movie. As we find ourselves becoming worked up, we remind ourselves, "Relax, it's just a movie," and the tension immediately subsides. We pull ourselves together by remembering that we are sitting in a chair fifty feet away from a screen watching actors work from a script. When considered from this perspective, it sounds a little crazy that a projected strip of celluloid can cause us to experience real physiological change due to serious emotions. Of course, getting pulled into the illusory drama is a big part of what makes a movie an enjoyable, compelling experience. The other critical aspect, however, is the realization that what's happening on the screen either isn't real or isn't actually happening to us. It is the existence of this space that allows us to truly enjoy the shock of a horror movie or the sadness of a tragedy. Without it, we'd lose perspective. Likewise, it is space that allows us to refrain from flipping out for thirty minutes just because we run into a traffic jam; it is space that allows us to keep from getting lost in drama, whether that drama derives from a fiction on a movie screen or an inconvenience or disappointment in our own lives.

When separation and space were present in my swing, ninety-five miles per hour fastballs seemed to come at me in slow motion and my bat seemed to be pulled through the hitting zone by an external force. Similarly, everyday issues lost their potentially overwhelming velocity when I viewed them from a distance and solutions came effortlessly from my deeper self (rather than from the shallower source of the mind).

When we don't think too hard in search of answers, they often appear out of space. Consider how it is often easier to give good advice to a friend with a problem than it is to figure out our own problems; this is because space naturally exists between ourselves and others and so we have a calmer, clearer vantage point. Still, even the most spiritually advanced lose themselves in the drama of daily life. Perfection is not the point. Rather, the key is to catch yourself early when you lose perspective. Meditating daily, we *observe* our minds, our egos, and our emotions from a distance, learning to watch ourselves as witnesses, no longer drowning in thoughts or emotions.

As a ballplayer, I was perceived as even tempered. This did not always work to my advantage with coaches, fans, and the press. Some coaches preferred fiery players. *Los Angeles Times* columnist T. J. Simers once referred to me as "the puddle" because of what he perceived as a lack of emotion. However, I just had a little more space and separation in my life than the guy who chucked his helmet after strikeouts. Being more emotional doesn't equate to caring more. I cared plenty, but even when dealing with a reporter as hypercritical as Simers, I practiced space. There were many guys on the team who either wouldn't talk to him or would scream at him. But those players tended to be consumed by their sense of identity and played right into his hand. He'd poke at their egos, knowing that if he touched the right nerve, they'd fill up his column with juicy material.

Finally, it was no coincidence that I found separation and space in my swing and in my life at the same time. My meditation not only improved my game, but also my ability to leave my successes and failures at the ballpark rather than always take them home with me. In the past, I often felt anxious and depressed. For example, for the first month of my rookie year I lived at SkyDome Hotel and after every game I'd return to my room and watch *Dumb & Dumber* on my Spectravision just to bring some lightness into my pressurized world. (Talk about having no space, I literally lived at the stadium!) In those days when I slumped at the plate my whole world slumped, and there were plenty of days I was unable to get out of bed until it was almost time to leave for the ballpark. Becoming a major leaguer had been a lifelong dream, but I didn't enjoy it those first three years. I had no separation from my successes and failures on the field. When I got hits I was happy; when I didn't I was depressed. My batting average those first years was not bad, about .285. Nonetheless, that meant I was happy only 28.5 percent of the time, and thus sad the other 71.5 percent. I needed the perspective of space.

And when I gained it I took off.

It was a packed Friday night against the New York Yankees, whose presence in any visiting ballpark in the late nineties cranked up the fire for both fans and players. Adding to the drama was that pitching for us was the defending Cy

Young Award winner, Roger Clemens, who brought heightened intensity of his own to our dugout whenever he took the mound. In my first at-bat against Ramiro Mendoza, I smoked a ball so hard off the top of the wall in left that outfielder Tim Raines was able to play the ricochet to hold me to a single. My next at-bat, I hit a home run into the second deck in right field. The game remained close into the seventh inning when Yankees manager Joe Torre instructed his left-handed pitcher Mike Stanton to walk our switch-hitter Tony Phillips in order to face me, opting to play the odds with a lefty-lefty matchup. I battled to a full count, then took the next pitch over the centerfield wall for a grand slam and my fifth RBI of the game. Against the best team in baseball my home run solidified a win for our ace pitcher and I'd come inches away from hitting three home runs—one to left, one to right, and one to center—which confirmed for me the power to all fields approach I'd developed in the BP game.

Yes, a skinny kid could be a power hitter.

AWARENESS

Thirty minutes after my break-out game against the Yankees, I stood at my locker in the SkyDome clubhouse surrounded by a half-circle of twenty or thirty reporters, each holding a microphone, camera, or tape recorder in my face. I picked out a question from among the shouted cacophony.

"Shawn, were you surprised Torre walked Phillips to pitch to you with the bases loaded?"

I glanced across the room, to where my teammate Pat Hentgen was watching with a grin. When I was a rookie, he'd advised me how to handle reporters: the more boring the answers, the fewer the questions. "Joe had little choice but to walk the switch-hitter to face me," I said. "He's a great manager and he had to go with the lefty-lefty matchup. It was the textbook move."

Next question:

"You've already surpassed your single-season career high of sixteen home runs and we're only in July. How do you explain this new power to all fields?"

The baseball world was starting to notice me. It felt good. Nonetheless, I responded with only half the truth. "In my first three years I only got to bat against right-handed pitchers," I said. "Now I'm playing every day, hitting in the top of the lineup." This was true, but it left out the core of my story—how just over a year ago I could barely get out of bed to face the struggles of a career hanging by a thread, how my daily meditation at the tee and the discovery of separation and space had altered my life, how I'd tapped into stillness to slow down my crazy world. Of course, none of that would have worked as a sound-bite answer for a locker room interview.

"What were you thinking during that last at-bat, Shawn?"

Now, this was an interesting question. The truth was that I hadn't been thinking anything at all. In the past, my awareness and attention had been confined to my swirling thoughts, but now they'd been set free from the entrapment of the mind. The game of baseball (and my world off the field) was becoming much clearer because I no longer confused my thoughts with my true essence. Still, I didn't offer this in answer to the reporters. Instead, I gave them only what they needed to fill their columns. "I was doing my best at the plate to battle and, fortunately, I managed to get enough wood on the ball to clear the fence."

Dan Millman's book *The Way of the Peaceful Warrior* discusses the power of losing your mind and coming to your senses. By the middle of the '98 season, I'd begun to truly understand what he was writing about. Before, I had always played the game through the filter of the mind, which is distorted by incessant judging and analysis. My awareness, clouded by fears of failure or illusions of grandeur, perceived only my mind's opinion rather than what was actually before me. I barely even noticed the pitcher on the mound! But now, separated from my obsessive internal world, I often felt like exclaiming to the pitcher, "Hey, what are *you* doing out there? I never noticed you before!" I revamped my swing, by moving my awareness into different body parts, and now I was able to move it even further from my mind to encompass the guy standing 60 feet, 6 inches away.

Some people do this instinctively.

I had to learn it.

Every day of that '98 season, I hit batting practice against our bench coach, Jim Lett. He was in great shape and took pride in throwing every pitch over the plate for fifteen minutes of rapid fire, allowing the batter no time to think. The only way I could hit at his pace was to focus all of my attention, leaving no room for any sense of myself; fortunately, my no-mind tee work complemented his style of throwing. Sometimes, we'd get into rhythms where he would throw every pitch right where I wanted it, and I would launch every pitch deep into the seats. We became locked into the *action of batting practice* and lost our individual senses of self. He wasn't throwing and I wasn't hitting, we both became the movement, just as dancers moving in sync become the dance rather than individuals dancing.

And then there was Tony Fernandez . . .

I was fortunate in batting practice to have been placed in a group that included Tony, whose awareness of his swing was as developed as anyone I ever saw. He was a wise, true master of hitting, and so I affectionately nicknamed him Yoda, though judging from his response I don't think he was much of a *Star Wars* fan. Every day in BP, Tony would join Carlos Delgado, Darrin Fletcher, and me for our fifteen minutes of work. Carlos always went first and was charged with watching the clock to make sure we all got the same number of swings. I followed Carlos, since he and I were going at it in our daily home run derby. Fletch went next, hooking balls down the right field line when he wasn't busy stirring the good-natured competition between Carlos and me. Tony Fernandez batted last. Patient and self-contained, Tony often seemed oblivious to whatever shenanigans were going on around him. He'd step into the cage and take his swings with complete attention on what he was doing. Tony didn't always use all his allotted time because he paid attention only to one thing—he'd hit until he felt his legs driving his swing in such a way that his bat came through the zone as if it were swinging itself. Some days, he'd walk into the cage and take only half of his swings and then stop because he'd found the feel he was looking for. Once in a while, he'd walk into the cage, take one perfect swing, and walk out. Without a word, he'd put away his bat and head directly into the clubhouse. Fletch, Carlos, and I loved when he did that because it meant we'd get extra swings. Soon, we encouraged him after every swing. "Beautiful swing, Tony . . . Your legs look perfect . . . Go ahead and take it on in to the clubhouse . . . What a great one to end on!" When he was in a playful mood, we'd catch a grin on the master's face. Other times, when he couldn't find his legs, he'd silence us with a glare. What a lesson Tony provided us, working with such awareness of his body and swing that he always knew exactly what he needed, nothing more and nothing less. One perfect swing was more valuable to him than eight or ten mediocre swings. He was all about quality and could care less about quantity.

Another lesson I learned from Tony was the importance of remaining calm, self-disciplined, and committed to one's own work standards even in the midst of a batting slump. For example, whenever Tony lost his feel for a few games, he'd bust out his long, heavy bats. Most guys grab a lighter bat when they're slumping to try and increase bat speed. Not Yoda. "When I use a bigger bat, it forces me to use my legs and body perfectly or else I won't be able to get it around," he explained. Tony wasn't one to put Band-Aids on his swing just to scratch out an extra hit or two when he was struggling; rather, he remained always committed to finding his true swing. If that meant going hitless for a game or two by swinging the heavier bat, he was willing. Tony knew his swing and he knew himself, and I was fortunate to have had a teammate whose approach to the game offered such lessons. His mere presence had a profound impact on my personal success.

By midseason '98, my connection to the pitcher began to make its way beyond BP and into actual games. I was no longer battling against a pitcher who was trying to get me out. I'd step into the box and, through my rhythmic routines, become aware of my body. Released of the mind's interference, my awareness (as unselfconscious as a predator striking its prey) was now free to connect to the pitcher.

By the time the ball left his hand, I was fully alert in the moment, so that the pitcher was now my partner in hitting rather than my opponent. Since there was no identifying with myself, what was left? Nothing, no one, only a single action, hitting. During my increasingly frequent hot streaks, I became the act of hitting rather than a person who was hitting. In the absence of any weighty sense of self, I'd step into the batter's box much lighter. Sometimes, I'd step out between pitches to revisit my mind. "Check the signs. What's the count? What's the game situation?" But as soon as my spikes returned to their toeholds, my mind would dissipate. My body would move through its routine, extending my awareness out to the pitcher. I'd feel my fingers wiggling around the bat handle and my body subtly rocking, but I'd be completely *out there*, at once anchored to my body and locked on the pitcher.

It was a whole new ballgame.

With this new acuity, I began to notice that many pitchers tipped their pitches. Much like experienced poker players who discern their opponents' bluffing by reading subtle gestures or changes in posture or facial expression, I began to note pitchers' tiny glove movements and differences in their deliveries to anticipate what they were going to throw. I'd been exposed to tipping as early as my days with Cito, but I'd been too lost in thought and analysis in those days to prosper from it. I'd step up to the plate with my analytical mind on overload; if I knew the pitcher was going to throw a fastball, I'd likely swing at it even if it was over my head or in the dirt. Entering the batter's box in a state of no-mind was a whole different story. I couldn't help but benefit from all the wonderful tells that pitchers provided me.

It's amazing what we notice when we actually watch with full awareness.

Now, when I knew what kind of pitch was coming, I no longer needed to swing at every fastball or alter my stride to hit an off-speed pitch. If I knew a changeup was coming, I didn't *think* about it—I simply *watched* for a slower pitch in a specific location. If the ball was in that location, the swing happened on its own. I wasn't thinking, just watching. Over the remaining ten years of my career, close to half of the pitchers I faced (including more than a few Hall of Famers) gave away their pitches.

One might think Major League pitchers should know better than to tip their pitches. After all, they're the best of the best. But Major League pitchers are actually more likely to tip than even high-school pitchers or Little Leaguers. This is because less experienced pitchers aren't likely to have thrown enough pitches to have ingrained consistent mechanics, whereas major leaguers throw thousands of pitches each year in the bullpen to recreate the same deliveries over and over. Every fastball they throw should be a mirror image of the previous fastball, every changeup a mirror image of the previous changeup, and so on. The more precise they can become with their motions, the more precise they will be with their pitch locations. Thus, as they do their work in the bullpen they reinforce the same movements. Unless a pitcher is aware that he tips and is trying to fix the problem, he gives little thought to the subtleties of his delivery. But I was paying attention to the subtleties.

The most common way pitchers tip is with their gloves.

Different pitches are held differently in the throwing hand. A fastball is gripped with the index and middle finger on top of the ball, whereas a changeup is gripped more with the palm. Thus, the hand holding a changeup often makes for a wider hand in the glove. As a hitter, I'd observe from sixty feet away the glove get bigger, or *flare*, by just an inch or so with this widened changeup grip. The movement didn't have to be drastic for me to pick it up and know what was coming.

One of the many pitchers who tipped in this way was the Minnesota Twins' Brad Radke, who was known for his top-notch changeup. My teammate Carlos Delgado, also adept at picking up these nuances, told me early in the year, "Watch his glove. He flares it on a changeup." I took note of this in a journal (there are too many games and too many pitchers to keep track of via memory). The next time I faced Radke, I saw his glove flare just after he nodded to the catcher's sign. He threw me a good changeup exactly where he wanted it, down in the strike zone—the pitch would have been tough for me to hit well if I hadn't known it was coming. As it was, I hit it for a home run off the clock in right-centerfield, just below the upper deck at the Metrodome.

Kevin Appier was a pitcher I'd never hit well until I discerned his tip. His approach was to get a hitter thinking inside fastball to speed up the hitter's bat, which subsequently made it almost impossible to lay off the next pitch, a slider or forkball that would break, unhittable, into the dirt. After I noticed that his glove popped open for a fleeting instant in the middle of his windup on both the slider and the forkball, while it remained skinny on his fastball, he became much easier to face. Skinny glove equals inside fastball. Glove popped open equals something else. The tip happened so fast and came so late in his delivery (not uncommon among the pitchers who tipped) that any distraction of thought would have paralyzed me as a hitter; there was no place in my awareness for my mind if I was going to see and respond to such subtle glove differences.

I faced Randy Johnson often. At first, his tip was easy to discern because, much like Radke, his glove flared before he began his windup. When Johnson, one of the top left-handed pitchers of all time, threw me his nastiest slider just off the outside corner and I didn't even flinch, let alone swing at it, he knew I had his pitches. He adjusted, and soon he no longer flared his glove on the slider while taking the signs. However, his habit was so engrained that as he turned sideways in the middle of his windup his glove would still pop open if he changed from his fastball grip. In one game, he grew so paranoid about us having his pitches that he altered his whole delivery by hiding his hand behind his back rather than keeping it in his glove as he normally did. I enjoyed seeing such an intimidating figure completely lost in his head. I hit nearly .300 against him with a couple of home runs, not bad considering that most lefties seemed to always come up hurt prior to games he was pitching. Nonetheless, he was so good that he still got me out 70 percent of the time even though I knew which pitch was coming! Without his tipping, I'd have had no chance.

Randy's lesser-known teammate, Armando Reynoso, exhibited a different but equally common manner of tipping his pitches. He didn't throw very hard, especially late in his career, so his bag of tricks relied on fooling the hitter. Thus, whenever he threw his changeup or curveball, his windup and delivery would be faster than when he threw his fastball, when his delivery noticeably slowed. Subconsciously, he'd try to sell the hitter that a fastball was coming by speeding up his delivery whenever he threw his changeup; conversely, he'd slow down his delivery whenever the fastball was coming in hopes of slowing the hitter. From the stretch, the difference was that the glove came set much faster on the changeup and slower on the fastball. One game, with runners on first and second, he came set with a medium tempo, leaving me uncertain as to what he was throwing. I called timeout. (I'd only ever call timeout on two occasions: one, if the pitcher was messing with a base-stealing teammate by holding the ball for a long time; two, if a tipper left me unsure as to what he was going to throw, whereupon I'd step out of the box to make him retip his pitch.) This time, Reynoso came set with his faster glove movements. My eyes popped open, even though my stare was already at full intensity. He floated a slow changeup right down the middle and I launched it deep into the seats for a three-run home run.

When it came to John Smoltz and Curt Schilling, as with Appier, only a handful of hitters in the league picked up the subtle tips of their pitches. Both guys threw hard, straight fastballs known as *four-seamers*, occasional *cutters* (fastballs that cut inside to a left-handed hitter), curveballs, and hard forkballs. They both threw fastballs at over ninety-three miles per hour, while their ninety miles per hour forkballs dropped into the dirt at the last second. When the ball came out of their hands, it was next to impossible to differentiate between fastballs and forkballs, which is what made them so effective.

Fortunately for me, I often knew *before* they released the ball whether a fastball or forkball was coming.

Schilling's glove started the same every time out of the windup, but when his glove went over his head, the fingers rounded on the forkball, and remained flatter on the fastball. From the stretch, it was more difficult to catch and I sometimes got crossed up because the differences were so subtle. Other times, I swung and missed even though I knew what was coming because Schilling had such good movement on his pitches. Meantime, John Smoltz, also a top pitcher of his era, tipped his pitches in a similar but slightly different manner. Before he started his windup, his glove was slightly flared on the forkball. It was so slight, however, that I was rarely completely sure. Fortunately, in the middle of his windup, the angle of his glove was horizontal on the forkball and diagonal on the fastball. Like Appier, this action was fleeting, and occurred so near his release that it was impossible for me to utilize unless I was devoid of all thought.

Among all the pitchers who tipped, Greg Maddux was my favorite to hit against. He was viewed as a professor of the art of baseball because he was such an intelligent pitcher. Somehow, he could always tell when a left-handed hitter was anticipating his trademarked, moving fastball, which started straight for the hitter's hip and then, at the last moment, ran back over the inside corner of the plate for a strike. So, instead of the fastball, he'd throw a nasty changeup. Meantime, he'd mix in cutters and curveballs, all to disrupt the hitter's timing. He knew that most hitters geared up their swings to unload on the ball when they got ahead of him in the count, so he'd defy their expectation by taking more off his fastball instead of throwing it harder. He didn't need to try hard to get hitters out, but let the hitters get themselves out.

I enjoyed facing Maddux because I felt he approached pitching in a similar manner to which I approached hitting. (Additionally, it's always fun facing one of the best.) It wasn't until a few years after I first faced him in '97 that I discovered he was tipping his pitches. The master was actually tipping! My teammates said, "No way, Maddux doesn't tip." But he did. Not only was I excited as a batter to have his pitches, but I felt as if I had won an unspoken chess match against Bobby Fischer. From the windup, when he stepped back to begin his motion and the glove went over his head, I noticed that I could see an inch of the palm of his throwing hand peeking out of the heel of his glove when he threw his faster pitches: the fastball and the cutter. When he was throwing his soft pitches—changeups and curveballs—I could barely see any of his throwing hand. As a hitter, I was more concerned with knowing hard or soft rather than whether a pitch was going to curve. I knew that if I could be on time for the pitch, then I could adjust to the movement of the ball.

I only had Maddux's pitches out of the windup. In a perfect world, I'd have had him in the stretch too because that would have meant there'd be base runners to drive home. Maddux was so good, though, it was rare for hitters to reach base anyway. Thus, he was in the windup more often than most other pitchers. And my at-bats against him when he was in the windup worked to set up the way he pitched me with guys on base. For example, if he threw me an inside fastball out of the windup that I laced into the right field corner for a double (in part because I knew what was coming), my next at-bat with a runner on base he'd likely to try to get me out with off-speed pitches. He still might show me fastballs inside off the plate, but he would shift his plan to off-speed pitches, playing into my hand.

Eventually, I became so adept at picking up tips, even from unknown pitchers, that I'd sometimes flash Carlos a quick sign as to what the pitcher was doing between pitches of my at bats. If a guy flared his glove on the changeup, I'd make eye contact with Carlos when I stepped out of the box and then subtly spread my fingers while holding my bat.

In a game against the Braves' left-handed rookie Bruce Chen, whom I'd never faced before, we were down four runs with the bases loaded when I noticed that his delivery was faster on his off-speed pitches and slower on his fastball. Next pitch, I hit a grand slam. As I touched home plate and high-fived Delgado, who'd approached from the on-deck circle, I mouthed to him, "Fast-slow, slow-fast." That was all he needed to know and he followed my grand slam with a homer of his own. As great as it had felt to round the bases with a game-tying grand slam—the crack of the bat, the roar of a big crowd, the arc of the ball, the circling of the bases, three teammates waiting with high-fives at home plate—it felt just as good to have deciphered the secrets of a new pitcher in real time and to have passed along that information, leading to Carlos' go-ahead home run.

And then there's Mariano Rivera . . . He never tips, though hitters know what's coming from him 95 percent of the time. No matter, I still couldn't hit him. He had such a devastating cutter that it didn't matter if hitters (especially lefties) knew it was coming. Pitch after pitch, he threw ninety-five plus miles per hour fastballs that seemed to jump up and in to lefties at the last possible moment. As the ball came out of his hand, it would look to be a strike on the inside part of the plate, but when I'd swing, the ball would be in at my knuckles. That's why lefty after lefty wound up running down the line with the handle of his bat in his hand, grounding out to the right side of the infield. Rivera was so good that I never brought a good bat up to the plate with me when I faced him because I didn't want to destroy a favorite piece of lumber.

In the late innings of an early season game in the Bronx against Rivera, I told my teammate Pat Hentgen that I was going to take every pitch. "It always looks like a strike out of his hand but then ends up inside," I said. "I'll just refuse to swing."

He laughingly gave his approval. "Good plan. It's never a strike."

I strolled up to the plate. The first pitch split home plate, straighter than a pitching machine could have thrown it. "Strike one!" the umpire yelled. I looked into the third-base dugout at old Yankee Stadium and saw Pat whispering something into teammate Chris Carpenter's ear. The next pitch was the same thing, right down the middle. "Strike two!" This time Pat held his hands up in the air with a big smile on his face. I was still determined to follow my plan even though the count was 0-2.

The next pitch was also straight and down the middle. I'd

intended to take it, but with two strikes I managed a useless, feeble swing (commonly referred to as an *excuse-me swing*). The ball was already in the catcher's glove as I made my half-wave of the bat. "Strike three!"

Who knows, maybe Rivera was reading my body language! Maybe I was tipping my approach by the way I was standing in the box. I'll never know, unless one day Mariano writes a book of his own.

The at-bat against Rivera illustrates in extreme terms the danger of approaching a pitcher by relying on guessing rather than on full awareness. I didn't go up to the plate with my full attention; instead, I went up there guessing with my mind rather than seeing with my eyes. That's no way to hit, it had left me paralyzed at the plate, ending in a three-pitch strikeout.

Carlos and I often talked about the way our own minds interfered with our at-bats. We viewed the phenomenon as being akin to the way Bugs Bunny is sometimes depicted with a whispering angel on one shoulder and a whispering devil on the other. Back in the dugout after freezing on a fastball down the middle of the plate for strike three, Carlos or I would dejectedly admit to the other, "The little man on my shoulder told me he was going to throw a slider." Going hitless for a couple of games could invite the little man in, putting my awareness back into my mind rather than where it belonged—on the pitcher. Rigorous travel could do it. Even off the field dramas could do it. The mind is always there, incessantly spinning its web of thoughts, and any moment of weakness can let it back into places where it is unwanted. There is a reason why meditation is referred to as a *discipline*. It takes constant practice and dedication to maintain separation from the mind. Fortunately, I realized that as long as I remained locked onto the pitcher's movements I could keep my awareness out of my mind. If I was on deck and the other team made a pitching change, I'd watch the new pitcher's eight warm-up pitches in a semimeditative state—full awareness. In the dugout, I watched just as intensely, and so instead of only connecting with the pitcher for the brief duration of my four at-bats each game, I could connect even during my teammates' at-bats.

Before that season, I wasn't even aware that a little man was ever on my shoulder, chattering and interfering. How would I know? Until I achieved separation from the mind, I'd known nothing *but* chattering. Still, even after I became aware of him, the little man continued to creep onto my shoulder from time to time. I'd hear his voice before the pitcher even looked in for a sign from the catcher. "Here comes a fastball, Shawn, on the inside part of the plate, hit it as far as you can," at which time I'd flail away at a slider in the dirt, having been so geared up by my mind that I lost control of my own actions. The little man is persistent, but I developed defensive maneuvers.

For example, I'd step out of the box and hit the sides of my cleats very firmly with my bat. Spectators probably thought I was mad at myself, but I was hitting my shoes to make my feet tingle, to feel my *feet*, to move my awareness into my feet, and out of my *mind*. From my body I could extend my awareness out to the pitcher, but I could never do so when my awareness was in my head. The master, Tony Fernandez, had a similar way of shifting his awareness. He'd tap with his fingers on his temples when he felt he wasn't seeing the ball well. He said the tapping stimulated the nerves that connected his eyes to his brain. While his physiological explanation may be suspect, his tapping undoubtedly served to connect his awareness to his body, specifically his eyes. This shifting of awareness to parts of one's body is a fast, simple way to get out of the mind.

Another way I'd get out of my mind while at bat was to pretend I was watching an exciting movie starring the guy on the mound, sixty feet, six inches away. The movie started with his windup and continued as the ball moved toward me. In this way, I could take myself out of the at-bat and simply watch. If the pitch was good, the swing just happened with no doing on my part. This movie-watching approach was all about keeping my attention on the pitcher and out of my mind and became one of my strongest assets.

I also came to realize just how haphazardly I had been watching as my teammates batted. I'd joke around with the guys in the dugout, flick sunflower seeds onto the field, or replay a previous play in my head. So, I didn't actually see much. Now, I watched the pitcher with complete attention whenever our left-handed hitters—Delgado, Fernandez, Jose Cruz, Jr., or Darrin Fletcher—were at bat, because pitchers were likely to use a similar repertoire of pitches for me. On the other hand, if a righty was hitting—Alex Gonzalez, Ed Sprague, or Shannon Stewart—I'd let up, watching with about the same positive attention as a fan sitting in the stands. After all, I couldn't remain hyperfocused for three hours straight. Besides, it's important in any endeavor to know when to focus and when to relax, when to joke around and flick sunflower seeds, and I was finally finding the right formula.

In time, watching allowed me to recognize pitchers' patterns and to understand how they were trying to pitch. I realized that when most pitchers are in doubt, they rely on their best stuff, rather than allowing a hitter's weaknesses to dictate what they throw. For example, sinker ball pitchers tend to throw sinkers when they need a ground-ball double play to get out of a jam, regardless of who's hitting. Besides, no pitcher has every kind of pitch to choose from. The fastball cutting inside gave me the most trouble, but not all pitchers had that weapon in their arsenal. Thus, I began to have a good idea as to what was going to be thrown even by pitchers who didn't tip their pitches.

In the past, my mind analyzed opponents pitch by pitch. Now, I regarded the at-bats as a whole. Separated from the mind, I could perceive more. Like a man standing in an art gallery looking at a painting by Seurat, I was now able to step back and see the big picture, to see what it was all about, instead of being so close that I could see only different colored dots of paint.

I began to keep a journal of individual pitchers' patterns, which over the years would get more high tech and develop into a simple database. Between at-bats, I'd run inside to my locker and jot down notes. I had tried something similar my first year in the league, logging each at-bat, pitch by pitch, but because I didn't yet know what I was doing, I'd wind up standing at the plate with my mind on fire: "Okay, last time he threw me a 1-1 slider, so he's probably going to do it again." And then he'd blow a fastball right by me. Rookie mistake. I'd learned the hard way that the old saying held true, "Analysis causes paralysis." However, by '98, I was ready to track pitchers in a more productive way. This time I made notes that helped me approach pitchers with a general plan, but *not* an analytical pitch by pitch plan. It was fluid. Sure, I used my mind to analyze the pitchers, but the analysis was done *after* the seeing, not during. I watched the pitcher with a quiet mind and only called upon my mind *between* pitches. Still, pitchers often confounded me, but I didn't have to be right every time. If I correctly anticipated one changeup in an at-bat or two or three pitches in an entire game, I was bound to have a lot of success over the course of a season.

I also realized that certain counts dictated pitch selections. As in other industries, baseball players follow trends. Some of the top pitchers of the '90s—Greg Maddux, Tom Glavine, Pedro Martinez, and others—had great success with their changeups to left-handed hitters, which they particularly liked to throw in hitter's counts, such as 1-0 or 2-1, when the hitters felt a little more aggressive. The pitcher didn't want to fall further behind in the count, but also didn't want to groove a fastball, knowing the hitter was ready to take his fiercest swing. So, he'd throw a changeup down the middle of the plate either to get an easy strike or to get a left-handed batter to hit the ball weakly to the right side of the infield. As these top pitchers succeeded with the approach, most of the league followed.

So, when I faced a pitcher who didn't tip his changeup, but nonetheless tended to throw it in these hitter's count circumstances, I'd watch for it. If he threw me a fastball instead, I'd just take it for a strike. Later, I'd likely find myself again in a hitter's count, and more times than not would get what I was looking for. I wasn't guessing; rather, I was following a plan that provided a few optimal pitches to hit each day. Sometimes I was wrong for an entire at-bat or for a whole game, but I was giving myself my best chance.

I even came to realize that many guys pitch differently with a base runner on second than they do with a base runner on third. In both cases, the runner is in scoring position. However, with a runner on second, pitchers don't have to worry so much about the hitter making contact, so to keep hitters off balance, pitchers tend to throw curveballs and sliders in the strike zone; with a runner on third and the prospect of simple contact resulting in a run, pitchers tend to throw more fastballs high and inside, as that's a pitch often popped up or fouled back. Also, many pitchers throw fewer forkballs with a runner on third, because they don't want to bounce one by the catcher. Others tend to throw the same pitch on a full count as they've thrown the pitch before, because they already have the feel for the pitch.

These are but a few of the countless scenarios I logged.

Still, each at-bat always unfolded in its own way. A checked swing or a 350-foot foul ball altered my game plan, because it was likely to have altered the pitcher's plan. My notes provided a general framework each game, but the ever-changing game situations forced me to stay present. I went up to the plate with general guidelines regarding a pitcher's tendencies. The pitcher still chose his pitches, but I felt I was in control because I had *my* plan. I waited for *my* pitch, not his. I didn't sit on pitches in the manner other hitters often describe, which involves too much guessing and effort. Rather, I wanted to approach pitches with stillness, patience, and no thought, just waiting, watching, and seeing. This allowed me to *respond* to pitches, as opposed to my first few years in the big leagues, when I merely *reacted* to pitches.

The difference between reacting and responding is subtle, but immense.

In a game against the Angels in Toronto, I faced Tim Belcher, a smart pitcher I'd seen many times and against whom I was hitting less than .200. Now, I focused on what I wanted to hit—any pitch on the outer half of the plate. Belcher knew I couldn't hit his inside cutter, so that day I decided to lay off any pitch that appeared to be over the middle of the plate (knowing it would likely break onto the inside corner). Some I took for balls and others for strikes, but I remained patient. Finally, he threw a cutter that stayed over the plate, and I responded by hitting it into the fifth deck of the SkyDome in right field. Only three other hitters had ever reached the fifth deck at that time: Jose Canseco, Joe Carter, and Carlos Delgado. I was no longer reacting but responding to each pitch in the manner that I wanted to.

Until the summer of '98, I'd approached hitting by just reacting to pitchers. My plan was simply to hit strikes and to take balls. If a pitcher threw a strike that was difficult to hit well (such as a curveball on the outer half of the plate), I'd swing at it even when I was ahead in the count and could have waited for a better pitch. Sure, I put a lot of balls in play, but I also wasted a lot of at-bats by hitting pitcher's pitches. I had no choice because I was living and playing each game only on the surface—I could only react to whatever came at me, whether it was a baseball or an issue off the field, because on the surface everything happens so fast there's no time to respond. Pitches coming at me . . . coaches breathing down my neck . . . the fans and media loving me, then hating me, based on my stats . . . So much surface distraction!

To become responsive, I had to move my awareness off the surface, to move deeper. This was not limited to baseball, but applied to my life off the field as well. Like many of us, I had falsely believed that the superficial dramas of my daily life defined who I was. Lost in my own story, I was like an actor who thought the character he was playing was reality. However, as I disconnected my awareness from my mind and emotions, the surface of my being, things changed.

Now, responding rather than reacting put me in control of my relationship with the pitcher. Common sense would tell you that the pitcher is always in control because he decides what pitch to throw, whereas the hitter isn't supposed to know what's coming. Of course, much of the time I did know what pitch was on the way, but even when I didn't, I was still often in control of my at-bats. This is because I knew which pitches *I* wanted to hit, so I simply watched for those pitches. I didn't sit on pitches or jump at pitches, as many hitters describe their calculated anticipation of a particular pitch. In my view, these practices rely too much on an effortful process of guessing and analyzing and reacting. I simply watched for pitches with no thought or action, just patiently waiting and seeing. And if I watched for my pitch with full attention, my swing happened spontaneously.

Just as opening my eyes to the pitcher enhanced my success at the plate, opening my eyes to the world improved my life. My meditative work at the tee was the initial vehicle by which I'd begun to know myself, and to realize that I wasn't an actor playing the role of Shawn Green, baseball player. Now, I was in touch with my deeper, true essence, which before had been lost in mind and emotion. The daily circumstances of life didn't change, pitchers didn't change, but my perspective changed and so now I could *respond* in my own way rather than merely *react* to both baseball and life. Now, my awareness controlled my life situations rather than life situations controlling my awareness.

I finished the '98 season, my first as an everyday player, with 35 home runs and 35 stolen bases, more than doubling both totals from any of my previous years. Under the tutelage of base-stealing legend Maury Wills, I became the first player in Blue Jays history to reach the 30-30 Club. Additionally, I topped 100 runs scored and 100 RBIs for the first time in my career. All these stats exceeded my wildest hopes from even a year before. And, more important, even on those nights when I went hitless I no longer felt the need to hunker down in my hotel room, watching *Dumb & Dumber,* anxious that my worth as a human being was defined only by what I had or had not accomplished on the field. The '98 season served not only as a breakout for my career, but also as a breakout from my mind.

That off-season, I jumped at the opportunity to see a bit of the world by traveling through Europe for a few weeks with Carlos Delgado. It was high time for me to take a break from my hard-driving life of public accomplishment, and time to cultivate the space between my true essence and Shawn Green, baseball player. Many people in their early twenties explore life before figuring out what path they want to pursue, whereas Carlos and I had both been signed to play baseball professionally as teenagers. Besides, we were young, unencumbered, and had a few bucks in our pockets. Why not enjoy the fruits of our labor?

So, we traveled through France, Spain, and Italy as tourists. Exploring other cultures and landmarks was a rich experience; however, equally rich was the effortless distance I discovered from my identity back in the States as a major league star on the rise. Other than a couple of Canadians who recognized us as ballplayers, Carlos and I were viewed no differently than any other pair of twenty-somethings travelling Europe. Maybe that's why people love vacation so much—it's an opportunity to separate from our other lives, our public identities. Sometimes, the awareness of this separation brings more joy than any particular destination.

I returned from Europe in late October and settled into my off-season lifestyle in Southern California. Like all professional athletes, I led two lives. During the season's brutal schedule of games, planes, and hotels, I lived as an adult with great responsibilities; during the off-seasons, when time was my own, I lived as a twenty-something-year-old kid who was largely indistinguishable from my lifelong friends.

I dated casually, but hadn't found love. Many people,

including teammates, told me I was lucky to be single in the big leagues and that, if they were me, they'd be having the times of their lives. That's not how I was wired. I longed for something deeper, something real. This had kept me always searching for that spiritual connection. Just as I had transcended the mind at home plate, I was now also beginning to find separation from it in my personal life. I suddenly understood that it was only my mind that dictated I seek a wife, just as it was my mind that continually said, "I'll be happy when . . ." or "I need this or that . . ."

The mind is closed and rigid, fixated on its desires; it manipulates all perceptions to fit into the paradigm it has created. Awareness, on the other hand, is open and fluid and offers a path to what is real. Awareness opened my eyes as a baseball player, enabling me to connect on the field, and now it was opening my eyes as a man, enabling me to connect to the world, to finally quit trying and to begin living. Pure awareness is wiser than the mind.

That winter, Lindsay was twenty years old and worked part-time for the surfwear manufacturer Quiksilver while she was going to school. A friend of mine and long-time employee of the company, Jacquie, had a plan to fix us up, arranging for me to come into the office on a Monday. The week before, however, I walked into a local taco stand to grab a quick bite and discovered a beautiful blonde standing in line in front of me talking with another young woman.

I made small talk.

Thankfully, it was a long line. When we got our order numbers to place on our tables, I asked the girls if they'd mind my sitting with them, since I was by myself. They looked at each other with a glimmer of flirtatious interest and half smirks that indicated surprise at my forwardness. (The little man would have reacted in the past, talking me out of such forwardness by giving me many excuses to chicken out. However, by having learned to circumvent my mind at the plate, my new, expanded awareness now flourished in all areas of my life and I could sense right away that Lindsay was someone special. Fully alert, all I had to do was respond to the situation.)

Lindsay stammered, "Sit with us? I *guess* so . . ."

I was already smitten by the light of her green eyes.

As we three ate our tacos, I asked where they worked. Lindsay said, "Quiksilver."

The lightbulb came on in my head, illuminating what my intuition had suggested when I first laid eyes on her. She was the one I was supposed to meet the following Monday. I debated whether to let her in on my little revelation or to surprise her a few days later when I showed up in her office. I opted to lay my cards on the table. "That's weird," I said, "a friend of mine is supposed to set me up with a girl there next week."

Lindsay smiled. "It's you?"

I'd found love when I stopped looking for it with my mind.

Signs and serendipities such as this began popping up everywhere for me after that. Why did it suddenly seem as if the world was guiding me through my journey, taking me by the hand?

This is why: I had learned to move out of my mind, which enabled me to see things that I had never before been able to see. My eyes were open to life for the first time and so I was immersed in the world. A year before, I'd been completely absorbed in developing my swing and my meditation at the tee. In the time since, I'd transcended my mind and connected with my true essence both on and off the field.

And now, to top it off, I'd effortlessly found the love of my life.

EGO

I entered the '99 season with a new sense of balance, happy to be exactly where I was. However, it hadn't been the reaching of key goals in my career and personal life that provided this happiness. After all, as soon as goals are reached the mind tends to immediately create a subsequent goal and then another and another, rarely ever satisfied. Rather, I was happy because I had gone beyond my mind and was able to simply enjoy the present, not obsessing about the future or the past.

And on the field it showed.

For the first time in my career, I got off to a hot start, finishing April with nine home runs and a batting average well over .300. Throughout May, I continued on a similar pace, hanging with the league leaders in home runs, batting average, and RBIs. Things couldn't have been better, but then the Yankees came to town.

I had my sights on making my first All-Star Game, but my chances were nearly shattered on May 28, thanks to an errant Andy Pettite fastball that broke a tiny bone in my left hand.

At first, I didn't know it was broken and headed to first base; I stole second on the next pitch, thinking, "If he's going to hurt me, I'm going to hurt his ERA by scoring a run." At the end of the inning, we returned to the field and it was then that I discovered I was unable to throw the ball.

A team doctor and a member of the training staff took me (in uniform, dirt and all) to the local hospital for an X-ray, and when they gave me the news I thought my chances of making the All-Star team had been demolished. In retrospect, I understand now that I'd have been wise to ask myself why such honors mattered to me so much. Now, I know I ought to have recognized my disproportionate disappointment as the emergence of my ego and taken heed of it as a warning of worse to come. At the time, however, I only knew I felt disappointed.

I left the hospital that night and grabbed a late dinner with one of our team's physicians, Glenn Copeland. Over the past few years, he'd become a close friend, as well as my medical advocate. I was in my twenties, with my entire family living on the other side of North America, so it meant a lot to me that he and his family treated me as one of their own, especially during the Jewish holidays. On this night, we settled into our booth at Gretzky's, a restaurant partly owned by the legendary Great One, and Glenn helped to soften the smarting pain of my injury, not so much from a medical perspective, but from an emotional one.

"This little injury won't slow you down at all, Greenie," he said. "You'll be out for about ten to fifteen games, and then you'll be back in the lineup as if nothing ever happened."

I shrugged. "Doc, I've dreamed of playing in the All-Star Game since I was five years old. If I miss too much time, I'll fall out of the league leaders in home runs and RBIs. I don't want to miss this chance."

"Torre will put you on the team either way," Glenn said. "You're having a great season."

I wasn't so sure. "You're forgetting how hard it is to make the All-Star team at my position," I said. "Most of the guys putting up big numbers are outfielders. There're a lot of great hitters to choose from."

Just then, the team trainer, Tommy Craig, walked up to our table. If anyone could cheer me up, it was Tommy (Glenn had told him to meet up with us after his work at the stadium was done). He greeted me with his nasal, almost incomprehensible Southern accent, "How's it feeling, Greenie?"

"Sore, but not too bad."

"Don't worry about it," he snorted. "You'll be swinging a bat again in a week. Besides, isn't that hot little girlfriend of yours coming out tomorrow? She'll nurse you back to health. When I first met her, I told Doc she was a keeper. Mark my words."

Tommy was right on all counts. Lindsay was coming to Toronto for the first time. Other than a couple of weeks together in Florida during spring training, she'd been exposed to little of my professional world—only my laid back, off-season lifestyle at the beach. I was excited to immerse her here in my other life. And, in light of my injury, she couldn't be arriving at a better time. Of course, her family was a little leery of her having given up a full-time job offer at Quiksilver to follow me around for the summer. But we were in love, and nothing was going to get in the way of that.

Glenn and Tommy and I hung out for another hour, eating a late dinner. Afterward, we headed to a nearby bar to meet up with Carlos, Alex Gonzalez, and a couple of my other teammates. We talked and laughed that night, and I thought to myself how lucky I was to have such great friends. And soon I'd have my girl in town. Sure, I was walking around with a broken bone, but life was still pretty damn good—it just took a little shift in my perspective to remember.

I missed only two weeks as a result of the injury, then picked up where I left off, reclaiming my position among the league leaders in several offensive categories. When Joe Torre selected his team, I got the nod. The All-Star Game, held at historic Fenway Park, was particularly memorable, as it was the last of the century, and featured appearances from most of the game's all-time living greats, including Ted Williams and Willie Mays.

Afterwards, my momentum at the plate continued and, spanning the entire month of July, I put together a 28-game hitting streak, the longest in Blue Jays' history (yet still only half of DiMaggio's famous 56-game streak!). Our team remained right in the wild card race up until the final three games of the year.

My '99 numbers finished up as follows: I batted .309 with 42 homers, 45 doubles, 20 stolen bases, 123 RBIs, and 134 runs scored. I was awarded both the Gold Glove and the

Silver Slugger awards, which recognized me as both the top hitter and the top fielder in my position in the American League. This success actually served to complicate my status with the Jays. The organization wanted to lock me into a long-term deal, as I'd be eligible for free agency after the following season. If I was unwilling to sign a long-term contract, they'd trade me to avoid the risk of losing me to free agency without getting anything in return. I had a decision to make.

As much as I loved my teammates and the fans in Toronto, it was time to move on.

At twenty-six, I didn't want to commit the prime of my career to a team that didn't seem capable of spending the money to acquire the talent necessary to win in the ferocious American League East. Also, at season's end, I learned that my three favorite coaches would not be back: Mel Queen, Jim Lett, and Sarge. I was also ready to try my hand in a larger market.

The circumstances of my contract allowed me to basically choose where I wanted to play. The Dodgers were my first choice. I liked the idea of coming home, playing in a big market, and the prospect of solidifying my relationship with Lindsay. In November of '99, the trade was completed. My agent, Jeff Moorad, negotiated a six-year contract totaling $84 million. Wow! Not only had I won the lottery, but I was coming home to play for one of the most storied franchises in baseball history. I received fond farewell phone calls from many of my teammates and coaches, two of which stand out in my memory.

The first call was from a guy I consider a class act and

sincere friend—Pat Hentgen. He was a pitcher who'd won the Cy Young Award in 1996, and had been a key contributor to the '92 and '93 world championship teams. I always admired the way he took the mound every fifth day, ignoring the kind of aches and pains that led to missed starts for many other pitchers. He was also a mentor to our talented young staff, including future Cy Young Award winners Chris Carpenter and Roy Halladay. Even though I was a position player with a different set of responsibilities, I often bounced ideas off him in the dugout between at-bats. He provided a pitcher's point of view, which was invaluable to me as game situations changed. My admiration for him extended to more than baseball alone. Four years my senior, he led the sort of life I aspired to; he was a good family man with a house full of children. His farewell call meant a lot to me. We talked for five to ten minutes as I sat on the couch with Lindsay at my home in Newport Beach. We said our goodbyes, and then he threw out a casual, "Love you, man," at the end of the call. None of my friends had ever said that, so I didn't know how to respond. He froze me in the same way that his big curveball so often froze hitters across the American League.

I just said, "Okay, take care Pat."

After hanging up, I explained to Lindsay what had happened. I thought she'd find it funny—she's got a great sense of humor. I explained to her, "There's no way to respond to a 'love you, man' from a friend. It doesn't sound right to say, 'love you too . . . man.' Am I right?"

I was laughing as I spoke, but she wasn't laughing as she listened.

She said, "Shawn . . . you pick that phone up right now and call him back and tell him you love him, too!"

"What?" I was shocked. "You're saying I should call him back and say, 'Hey Pat, it's me and I forgot to say that I love you too'? You're crazy, Lindsay!"

"But he put himself out there and you left him hanging," she said, half pleading and half laughing. By now, she knew she wasn't going to win this discussion.

"I don't think he's going to lose any sleep over it, babe."

We both still laugh about that; it was like something out of *Seinfeld* or *Curb Your Enthusiasm*. Lindsay is an old soul, someone who gets it. I'd been attracted to her at first because she was beautiful, but I fell in love with her for this kind of sweetness and depth.

Before we had even finished laughing at the awkwardness of the "I love you, man" situation, the phone rang again.

"Hello?" I said, picking up.

"Shawn . . ."

I immediately recognized the grizzly voice on the other end of the line: It was the coach who knew me best, Mel Queen. An old-school, salty baseball man, Mel was in his late fifties and had spent most of his years in professional baseball. As a player with the Cincinnati Reds in the late '60s, he'd been converted from an outfielder to a pitcher without ever being sent down to the minors to learn his new craft. As a result, he knew baseball from all angles and was the wisest coach I ever knew as a professional. Along the way, he groomed Cy Young Award winners Pat Hentgen, Chris Carpenter, and Roy Halladay (not to mention Roger Clemens, who won the award both years Mel was his pitching coach), and he developed numerous All-Star position players as well, including Jeff Kent and Delgado. He was the one coach whose opinion I always listened to because he was more *aware* than others as he watched the game.

"Shawn, let me tell you something and listen closely."

Mel had taken me in as a raw nineteen-year-old and groomed me for three years in the minor leagues as well as four of my five years in the majors. Now, over the phone, he spoke with the same no-nonsense tone he'd taken with me back at the minor-league practice facility in Dunedin, Florida, whenever I misplayed a ball in the gap. "Look Shawn, you just signed a ridiculously large contract and you're heading into a much bigger market than Toronto. Not to mention, you're going to have to deal with the difficulties of playing at home in front of all of your friends and family. Critics are going to be watching your every move. The minute you go zero for ten, you'll have microphones in your face demanding answers. With the kind of money you'll be making and with the numbers you put up the past couple of years in Toronto, you've set the bar very high. So let me give you one final piece of advice while I'm still sort of your coach."

"Of course, Mel," I responded. He was more than a coach to me, having groomed my game from the day I signed as a professional. "You know I always appreciate your advice."

His words are etched in my memory. "Don't change the way you approach the game, Shawn. Don't try to be the hero. Don't feel like you need to live up to anything you've done in the past or to the expectations everyone has for your future. Just play the game. Take each pitch one at a time. Things may be different all around you, but remember the game is still the same."

"Thanks, Mel. But I think I've got all that under control."

There was a long silence. At last, he said: "Okay, I'll be watching you. And even though we'll be wearing different uniforms don't be afraid to call me any time."

After the call, I thought about Mel's words. Good advice, as always. But wasn't it stuff I already knew? Over the last couple of years, hadn't I already figured out enough about myself, my life, and the game of baseball to avoid the pitfalls that Mel warned against?

I concluded that Mel was a great mentor and friend, and thus just hadn't been able to keep from being a bit overprotective.

After all, I was on top of the world. What could possibly go wrong?

A year later, a world away . . . a lot had gone wrong.

I walked toward home plate in San Diego for my last at-bat of what had been a long, disappointing 2000 season with the Dodgers. I knew that if I could reach the bleachers one more time I might yet salvage some small vindication for my first year in Dodger blue. My name rang out over the PA system, and I glanced up to the Qualcomm Stadium scoreboard: batting average of .269 with 24 HR and 99 RBI. With two men on base, one home run would round my stats up to .270 with 25 HR and 102 RBI, and the critics (myself included) would have to admit, "Well, that's not such a bad first year for a guy switching leagues," rather than, "Wow, the

Dodgers spent all that money on a guy who didn't even hit .270 or drive in 100 runs . . . what a mistake!"

Over the past year, my statistics had come to define my sense of self. Not good. I dug in against the Padres' Trevor Hoffman, one of the best closers in baseball. Like a junkie, I needed a home run and any perceptive observer could see by my jumpy, overanxious strides that this desire would dictate my last at-bat (as it had too many other at-bats throughout the season). I'd lost separation from my desire, my mind, and my emotions, all of which added up to the loss of separation from my *ego*, a term I use here to mean "one's consciousness of one's own identity," rather than "an inflated feeling of pride in one's superiority to others." Full of expectations, I lost my ability to *be* the act of hitting, the essential ingredient of my success in Toronto. This is why as I dug in against Trevor Hoffman I was consumed by thinking: "All I need is one more home run, and then I'll be happy."

The little man on my shoulder, who'd returned months before, whispered into my ear, assuring me that I needn't settle for knocking in the runners but could surely hit that twenty-fifth home run, a difficult chore with Hoffman, who was smart and aware on the mound. The little man continued whispering: "He's going to throw a first pitch changeup to get ahead with runners on base." Instead, Hoffman threw an eighty-nine miles per hour fastball right across the plate. Strike one. The next pitch was another fastball and I lunged anxiously at it. Crack! The ball headed down the right field line, far enough to be a home run, but hooked foul. Strike two. All year, my jumpy, lunging stride had caused me to pull balls. Now, I was 0-2 against a tough pitcher, and it was time to just put the ball in play and settle for the 100 RBI mark. Hoffman came set and threw a changeup, too close to take with two strikes. I swung feebly and grounded to the third baseman, who threw me out at first. My season was over—I'd failed. What a miserable, yet appropriate, way to end the 2000 season.

After saying my goodbyes in the clubhouse, I threw everything into my bag, grabbed a box of bats, and headed out to my car. I looked forward to separating from baseball for a while and getting back to working on my relationship with Lindsay, which was another aspect of my life that had gone rocky during that first year with the Dodgers. I pulled out of the stadium parking lot and made my way north on Interstate 5, my foot heavy on the gas. I wasn't focused on driving. Instead, I was lost in my chaotic mind, until a rapidly approaching sea of taillights at the border patrol checkpoint at Camp Pendleton jerked me back to the present. I hit the brakes hard.

My heart pounded.

There's nothing like a frightening moment to bring you back in touch with your body. Actually, it was the best I'd felt all day, as if the universe was shaking me out of a deep sleep. The Sunday evening traffic slowed to a crawl, then stopped. Suddenly, I could feel my hands on the steering wheel and my foot on the brake pedal. I looked around and began to see the world again. I no longer felt the need to be home but was fine being just where I was. And from a place much deeper than my mind a realization hit me: I had played the entire 2000 season in the same manner I'd just been driving the car—hurried and distracted.

Alone now, with idling traffic all around me to enforce a sense of stillness, I thought back on the season.

After finding stillness, space and separation, and awareness in Toronto, I had fallen victim to the temptation of building a new identity in Los Angeles. Every day of the just-completed season, I'd remained aware of my numbers lingering below my new—if imaginary—statistical bar. By signing that big contract and entering the huge Los Angeles market, I'd felt as if I was promising the organization, the fans, and the media that I would always match or exceed my best numbers from Toronto. Weren't numbers what they were paying me for?

I had approached hitting this past year with one eye on where I'd been and the other on where I wanted to be, leaving no attention for the present moment. I'd rush through each at-bat, trying to get a hit or, better yet, a home run, as quickly as possible in order to compensate for what was a perpetual sense of insufficiency. Even my sessions at the tee were no longer focused in the present moment but on trying to find my swing so that I could improve my statistics in upcoming games. Bad things happen when one's attention slips away. In the car racing up Interstate 5 I'd been daydreaming about the recently completed, miserable season, feeling full of regrets and irritation, and I'd almost driven myself into the back end of a truck. How had I come to this?

As if in answer, Mel Queen's words popped into my head: *Be yourself . . . Don't feel like you need to live up to anything you've done in the past, and don't feel like you need to live up to the expectations everyone has for you in the future. Just play the game.*

Intellectually, I'd understood what he was telling me, but it seemed now I'd been unable to heed the wise advice without first experiencing its opposite. I had read *Siddhartha* by Herman Hesse many times and thought now of Siddhartha's words: "Wisdom is not communicable. The wisdom which a wise man tries to communicate always sounds foolish . . . Knowledge can be communicated, but not wisdom. One can find it, live it, be fortified by it, do wonders through it, but one cannot communicate and teach it." I needed to live it.

It would have been easy to say to myself, "I must have been a fool not to have seen this coming." However, the first signs of my encroaching ego were subtle and seemingly harmless. In my final season in Toronto, I'd enjoyed the moment and relished my growth both as a player and a person; nonetheless, my growing self-identity must have been noticeable enough for Mel to have felt the need to warn me about it. I had underestimated his warning because I made the mistake of equating ego only with the grossly self-important attitude of many top athletes. I thought I was safe from the ego because I was a "humble guy." Even at the top of my game, I often stood in right field in front of 50,000 fans thinking, "I can't believe these people actually buy the fact that *I* am a major leaguer!" I always felt as if I had tricked everybody into believing I was someone special, someone to be admired. And I wasn't the only player who felt like that. A common response among ballplayers when asked how they're doing is, "I'm just trying to trick 'em for as long as I can!"

And then I arrived in Los Angeles.

In my mind, I ran through the just completed season, looking for clues:

At the November '99 press conference to announce the signing of my new deal with the Dodgers, I became a different player in the eyes of fans, press, management, and (foolishly) myself. I felt embarrassed that day by all the attention and, even more, by the huge new contract. Unlike many athletes, I was not driven to be among the highest-paid players in the game. I'd grown comfortable in Toronto as a rising star, but now I knew I was expected to be the major-market franchise player and returning hometown hero. Of course, I could see now that I ought not to have allowed the money and attendant expectations to distract me. The only part of my new contract that should have mattered to me was that I was going to be wearing a different uniform and playing in a different city. My approach to the game should have remained the same as in Toronto, where I'd grown adept at playing in the moment, while avoiding the pressures of the past and future. However, even as early as the press conference, the embarrassment I felt indicated I was giving it all too much importance, setting myself up for failure.

The first reporter raised his hand. "Shawn, with this contract, the Dodgers are investing a lot for you to lead them back to the World Series. Are you ready to relieve this city's disappointment of the last few years?"

Relieve the disappointment of an entire city?

My answer did not indicate my misgivings at such lofty expectations. Instead, I played along with the game, as I believed I was obliged to do. "Definitely," I said. "I'm coming to LA because I know this organization is dedicated to winning." The team had great players: Gary Sheffield, Kevin Brown, Eric Karros, and Chan Ho Park, among others. What

I really wanted was just to come in and do my part, to be one of the guys, but I knew my contract was going to make that difficult.

"Do you feel any extra pressure playing within an hour of Tustin, the city where you went to high school?"

"No, I'll just have to leave a lot more tickets for my friends and family this year!"

Another reporter turned the talk to numbers. "You were great with the Blue Jays last season, especially the forty-two home runs. But Toronto is a hitter-friendly park, whereas Dodger Stadium is more of a pitcher's park. What kind of numbers do you expect to put up next season?"

Any time home runs were mentioned, the little man on my shoulder tempted me to trouble. I loved hitting the ball farther as a skinny guy than most of the body-builder types in the game. "Oh, I'm not worried about the ballpark," I said, aware that I was expected to project confidence, even if it risked seeming like arrogance. "I plan to put up power numbers similar to my last two years in Toronto."

The next reporter's question upped the stakes even more. "So, Shawn, you're the most important Jewish player in the big leagues since Sandy Koufax. How will it feel to wear the same uniform he wore?"

Being mentioned in the same breath as a baseball legend, the most famous Jewish athlete ever! What an honor, what a weight. "I just hope I can play the game with as much class and integrity as he did. Of course, he's one of our game's best pitchers and the greatest Jewish athlete of all time, so I shouldn't be placed on the same level as him."

The reporter nodded, but the pressure was on, not only

from the press and fans, but, more dangerously, from within me.

That was only the beginning. A few weeks later, *Sports Illustrated* contacted me to do a big article on my move to Los Angeles. The story was to center on my being a Jewish athlete. They set the photo shoot at a well-known Jewish landmark in Los Angeles—Canter's Deli on Fairfax. This wasn't my first association with a Jewish deli. Back in '96 while playing a series against the Yankees, someone at 2nd Avenue Deli took a picture of me holding a big salami as if it were a bat, and they hung the photo on the wall.

At Canter's Deli I got a clear picture of what a big deal it was for a Jewish athlete to come to Los Angeles as a major sports star. People in the restaurant wished me luck and told me how proud they were to have a Jewish player leading the Dodgers. Even the hobbling, seventy-year-old waitresses conveyed their excitement. And every conversation asserted that I was the "next Sandy Koufax," an intimidating comparison not only on a baseball level but also because I hadn't actually been raised in a religious household. I'd never gone to Hebrew school and thus never had a bar mitzvah. (I had learned most of what I knew about my religion and Jewish heritage as a player in Toronto, where the Jewish community welcomed me.) Arriving in Los Angeles, I could only hope I was ready to embrace the label of Jewish role model.

What had become of stillness, separation, awareness?

The degree to which I allowed my new role as Dodger messiah to take hold of me became more evident a few weeks prior to spring training during a home run exhibition in Las Vegas. ESPN had decided to bring back a version of the old TV show *Home Run Derby*, which aired in 1959 with legendary sluggers like Mickey Mantle, Willie Mays, Hank Aaron, and Duke Snider. This new version, known as *Big League Challenge*, featured twelve of the top home run hitters from the '99 season. I'd be competing head-to-head, tournament style, with Barry Bonds, Mark McGwire, Jose Canseco, Manny Ramirez, and Alex Rodriguez, to name a few. And, for the first time, I'd be hitting as a Dodger. Since the competition was in Las Vegas (just a four-hour drive from Los Angeles), there were plenty of Dodger fans in the stands. My first round match-up was against the ultimate anti-Dodger and future owner of both the single season and all-time home run records—Barry Bonds.

Unlike the popular Home Run Derby held each summer prior to the All-Star game, this competition worked inning by inning. Each batter took turns, as in a regular baseball game. Any swing that didn't result in a home run was an out. The *Big League Challenge* producers hoped to create light-hearted, head-to-head competition and bantering. Most players act as if they don't care how well they perform during these exhibitions, but trust me, players care; I know my ego wanted to show off. Besides, with thousands of fans in the stands and other top home-run hitters watching, no one wanted to embarrass himself.

In Toronto, during my daily BP home run derby with Carlos, we took our biggest swings with a disciplined, up-the-middle approach that improved our power to all parts of the field. Sure, we enjoyed our little competition and trash talking, but our egos always took a back seat to our work, which consisted of developing our swings.

On the other hand, the *Big League Challenge* was all about ego. I stood at the plate as an ego, trying to impress while worrying about embarrassing myself. I cared nothing about honing my swing, only immediate results, and so I tried to hook everything to right field, the very approach that I'd rejected so dramatically years before when Cito Gaston and Willie Upshaw insisted I adopt it. Centerfield at this Triple-A ballpark, Cashman Field, was over 430 feet away, so there was little chance I could win the competition by aiming out there. I stepped up to the plate against Bonds and thought to myself, "How much damage can I do by spending one weekend trying to pull home runs?"

Standing at the plate at a minor league stadium in Las Vegas in a meaningless competition I completely succumbed to my ego. Unfortunately, this set the tone for my entire 2000 season, not so much because two days of pulling the ball actually destroyed my swing, but because I allowed my ego to take over my hitting. Suddenly, I was no different than most of the Vegas tourists who filled the casinos a few miles away on the Strip, which, after all, was built on egos driven to chase money in an attempt to find fulfillment. I was in Vegas not to chase money but home runs and, during the upcoming season, I'd continue to chase them in an attempt to live up to expectations. It was no consolation that I ended up beating Barry Bonds that day. Not when I weighed the victory against what I was about to lose.

Isn't that always the way it is when we win a game but lose ourselves?

After Vegas, spring training rolled around and I felt like a lonely kid who'd just changed schools and longed for his old friends. With the Jays, the focus of training camp had been always on baseball, with a smattering of public-relations chores. With the Dodgers, I bounced from interviews to photo shoots to promo videos to commercials, until the PR commitments became almost as demanding as the actual workouts. I was supposed to be the new star of Hollywood's team, and all the attention served to remind me daily of my new role as the forty-plus homers-per-year Jewish player who would turn around one of the most storied franchises in all of baseball.

Tommy Lasorda, Mr. Dodger, started in on me from day one. "Hey, Shawn, let me tell you something. If I asked God to send down the perfect player to wear this Dodger uniform, you'd be the guy he'd send."

I knew Tommy was given to hyperbole. Nonetheless, I also knew that the organization really had been searching for a new face since Mike Piazza left in '98. Gary Sheffield was an established superstar, but he was too outspoken for management's liking. They wanted someone to project a squeaky-clean image, and I was their guy. One morning at camp, Tommy upped the ante by showing up with one of the most legendary hitters of all time, a personal hero to me— Ted Williams. The Splendid Splinter was in a wheelchair and, as Tommy wheeled him toward my locker, he said to Ted, loud enough for everyone to hear: "Here's the young guy we were talking about. He's the modern-day version of you."

I held my hand out and said, "It's an honor to meet you, Mr. Williams." As a kid, there'd been two Hall of Famers I'd dreamed of meeting: Ted Williams and Sandy Koufax. In my first few days of camp, I'd met both (Sandy occasionally stopped by to help with the pitchers).

Ted shook my hand and said, "I like the way you swing

the bat. You generate good bat speed with your hips, similar to the way my swing used to work."

I didn't know what to say. I was awestruck by his presence and a little intimidated by his comparison (old scouts used to say my swing reminded them of Ted Williams's—the ultimate compliment—but it's one thing to hear it from them and another to hear it from the man himself!).

I was the man God would send to save the Dodgers? I had a swing like Ted Williams's?

Of course, I knew these were not just compliments but also exaggerations. Nonetheless, during spring training I couldn't help but embrace the idea that it was my responsibility to deliver on just such impossibilities. I came to believe that it wasn't going to be enough to be just myself. Ted Williams, Sandy Koufax, God's ideal Dodger . . .

Despite the pressure, the 2000 season got off to a good start from a statistical perspective. By the end of May, I was hitting .337 with 10 home runs and 39 RBIs. Still, I knew my swing was rushed and that it lacked separation and space. Further, I knew that the weight of my new identity as a superstar in Los Angeles was distracting me from the full awareness with which I'd played in '99. My reliance on fundamental mechanics at the plate would see me through only for so long. . . . Nonetheless, I convinced myself to put more weight on the good numbers than they deserved. "This is great!" I thought. "I'm hitting over .330 with plenty of RBIs and I haven't even found my groove yet. I'll really take off once I do!"

I made the mistake of allowing the numbers to distract me from the deeper truth I should have recognized about my rushed swing. Those first two months, I'd been getting hits for two reasons: First, the basic mechanics of my swing remained almost as efficient as they'd been the previous two seasons in Toronto; second, I'd been getting a little lucky and balls were finding holes through the infield (such good fortune can only last for a short time). The truth remained that my timing was off. That crucial space created by the slight pause between the landing of my stride and the forward movement of the bat was a nanosecond too short. My anxious desire to live up to my new role had sped up my swing just enough for my top hand on the bat to roll over the other hand at the point of contact rather than *just after* contact. This created topspin on the batted ball as opposed to the desired backspin, transforming homers into either doubles or outs. By June, my awareness either was going to settle calmly into the moment, allowing me to regain the space and timing in my swing, or my home run driven overanxiousness would affect the rest of the season.

The pull of my ego proved too strong.

My awareness became lost in my new identity. Fans and media sang my praises and I purchased a house in Pacific Palisades to immerse myself in LA culture. I thought I could achieve separation in my swing without having to first find separation from this overpowering identity. Wrong. What I didn't realize was that it was my ego that was pulling me out of the present moment at the plate. Instead of becoming the act of hitting, as I had in the past, I was working toward the purpose of fulfilling statistical goals.

I calculated that I needed to hit about 7 homers and notch about 20 RBIs each month to stay on track with the player I was supposed to be: the star who'd hit 42 home runs and had 123 RBIs the season before. Every time I stepped up to the plate I brought my statistical goals with me, and numbers have no place in the present moment. My statistical aims were mere fantasies of how the future *should* be, based on what I did the previous year. Living for the future while thinking about the past.

Where's the presence in that?

Likewise, my relationship with Lindsay began to suffer. My hitting wasn't the only thing the move to LA threw slightly off. At first, Lindsay and I maintained the momentum from our previous year in Toronto (it had been fresh and exciting to be together in a beautiful, foreign city, thousands of miles from California). There, it had been all about baseball, a few friends, and the two of us. It was perfect. In my naiveté, I had thought that coming home to play for the Dodgers would only make our relationship simpler; after all, Lindsay could retain her independence throughout the summer and I could live in one home rather than two. But this wasn't to be.

Now, Lindsay spent hours commuting between her Newport Beach apartment and my Pacific Palisades home, which was a long, stressful drive even without traffic. (She wasn't willing to move in with me before our getting engaged.) Another complication was that suddenly we had our families and friends continually tugging at us. And, because of my big contract and my technically single status, Lindsay had to deal with articles in LA publications depicting me as one of the city's most eligible bachelors. In short, she was being overlooked and I was too focused on hitting my statistical goals to notice. Desperate for answers, we both took to comparing where our relationship was now to what it had been the happy year before. In this way, we began chasing the past in the same manner I was chasing home runs. And all we managed to discover in the gap between how things were and how things should be was frustration, which led us to a painful split at just about the same time my impatient and distracted swing led me to the inevitable slump.

The space in my swing, slightly off in April and May, worsened in June. Daily, I grew more frustrated as the batted balls stopped finding holes and as I continued to mishit pitches that I used to launch into the bleachers. Still, my swing wasn't so far off from the previous year, I was one disciplined week away from slowing everything down and recreating the necessary space and separation. However, my obsession with chasing after imaginary numbers wouldn't allow me to return to a place of presence. I knew what my wise, former teammate Tony Fernandez would have done. He'd have grabbed his ultraheavy 36-inch, 36-ounce bat for about a week's worth of games and forced himself to hit with separation. I saw him do that even when he was hitting .400! He was never fooled by stats but remained always focused on taking perfect swings. Every time he pulled out those huge logs, we'd laugh and say, "Oh, no, Tony can't find his legs! He's bringing out the big bats!" But it worked. By swinging a heavy, long bat, he *had* to start his stride early. He *had* to create the proper separation and space so that his entire body could pull that log through the strike zone. He didn't care that using an oversized bat might cost him a few hits for the week that he used it. He was dedicated to finding the right feel, the right swing, regardless of the numbers. I hadn't been as wise as Tony. I wasn't willing to sacrifice my numbers for a few games in order to get it right. I was too connected to stats and the opinions of others. Besides, I still thought I had it all figured out. One day it would just click, right?

Wrong.

By the end of May I had 10 home runs, which put me on pace for 30 for the season. Not bad. The truth was that, as a young player, I'd have been happy to hit 20 or 25 per year. But now my identity was that of a 40-plus homer guy. Besides, players, coaches, fans, and media love home runs. Nike ran a humorous commercial with pitchers Tom Glavine and Greg Maddux working on their swings and saying, "Chicks dig the long ball!" Truthfully, nothing encouraged the overbearing distraction of my ego more than my being a home run hitter. The physical act of hitting a home run feels incredible. Even in batting practice, there's nothing like the feel of a perfectly timed swing; as the concentration of all of one's energy and power is transferred into the ball to send it soaring, it's intoxicating. The body feels so alive. In games, the home run hitter gets to take a slow victory lap amongst thousands of screaming fans. How can that not tug at the ego?

Entering June, my ego insisted I catch up with my home run pace from the previous season, but chasing home runs is anathema to finding a good groove—a hitter's stride gets jumpy and his swing gets both faster and slower. That's right, faster *and* slower!

How is that possible?

Everything the home run obsessed hitter does, beginning with the stride, becomes rushed, until you're jumping out to meet the ball almost before the pitcher releases it. Inevitably, you chase a lot of bad pitches. Additionally, when you try too hard to hit for distance, you often rely on your upper body rather than your legs to generate the power. Subsequently, the path of the swing becomes longer and so, even as your body moves more rapidly, the bat actually moves more slowly. I knew all this, but it didn't matter. My desire for more home runs became an obsession. I *needed* to hit 10 homers in June to get back on pace for 40. I approached every game like a junkie searching for his next fix. "Home runs, home runs, home runs . . ." was all I could think about, even when I wasn't at the stadium. My swing fell apart. Not only did I manage a measly 2 homers that month, but my batting average dropped 30 points. And even my ability to read pitchers' tendencies and pick up tips was compromised. After all, those skills had arisen only when my awareness was out of my mind and connected to the pitcher. Now, the little man was running the show again. Once again, I was guessing what pitches were coming next, seeing the pitcher through my mind's eye rather than seeing the reality of what was unfolding before me.

By July, with my home run total down and my batting average dropping, the coaches and media began to push the panic button. Because I was no longer responding to the pitcher but had returned to merely reacting, every pitch appeared to come at me at one hundred miles per hour. I didn't have *time* to respond. Each night at the plate, I rushed through at-bats, hitting tough pitches in counts when I should have been more patient, grounding out to either the first or second basemen. Sure, I hit plenty of balls hard. Some of my teammates told me what bad luck I was having. "Man, you're making so many hard outs!" I knew the opposite was true. Actually, I'd been getting by on a run of good luck the first two months and now I was back to reality: a flawed swing.

I already understood what some players never figure out; baseball is a perfectly designed game. If a player has great mechanics, with separation and space in his swing, then the balls he hits will find the holes even if he doesn't hit them as hard as others who have inferior mechanics. There's a reason why Hall of Famers such as Rod Carew, Tony Gwynn, and Wade Boggs managed to chop so many grounders between the third baseman and shortstop for base hits. They didn't have to hit the ball harder than others because they hit it better. By the time the All-Star Game (which didn't include me) rolled around in mid-July, I was swinging to hit my numerical goals rather to simply hit the ball. I was swinging to reach the future rather than the present. In the process, the present was lost, along with any chance of playing up to my potential.

I was a mess!

All of my growth over the previous two seasons had been undermined, as my attention turned from the present moment to an illusory image of who I was supposed to be. I'd lost the ability to find the stillness and meditation even during my tee work, as those sessions had transformed into a daily, desperate search for results.

My obsession with trying to live up to a new image carried over into my relationship with Lindsay. I was preoccupied, stressed, and irritable, and I lost track of her needs and the needs of our relationship. We temporarily split up twice that summer, once in late-May and once at the end of July. At those times, I found myself sitting alone in my new house, just as I used to sit alone in my Toronto apartment during my early career struggles. Sure, I was now in a fancy, five-thousand-square-foot palace in a neighborhood filled with celebrities, instead of huddled inside my old eight-hundred-square-foot apartment, but it felt even worse! The decor was great (my sister Lisa and friend Armida had decorated the house while I was away at spring training), the television was huge, and the pool beautiful. But I never stepped in the pool and I rarely made it down the stairs to watch the big television. I was having trouble getting out of bed, dreading the drive to the ballpark. Huddled in my big house, I could only think about what a mess everything was with Lindsay *and* with baseball.

The truth is that I resented the huge contract, which was all about my past and future and, along with the hoopla surrounding my move to the Dodgers, had tempted me out of living my life and playing the game in the present moment. Still, the big numbers on the contract weren't, in themselves, the problem. Nor were the disappointing stats displayed on the scoreboard every at-bat. Analyzing players by numerical comparison is inescapable. And whether one swings a bat for a living, sells widgets for a corporation, or is a high school student hoping to score high on the SATs, analysis and comparisons are inevitable and not without value. Numbers aren't the problem. The problem is losing oneself in numbers.

As my season spiraled downward, I fell further away from what I truly had come to love best about hitting, which was that I could lose all sense of myself in its practice. In Toronto, it hadn't mattered if I was hitting off the tee, playing the BP home run game, or hitting in an actual game; I *loved* to swing the bat because my ego was left behind. Now, swinging the bat had become a joyless activity because I had gotten lost in my ego's needs.

Of course, it's not uncommon to make the mistake of comparing where we are in our lives to where we should be. The truth is that there is no such thing as where we should be; we are where we are, period. Nonetheless, our culture provides limitless illusory images of what our lives should be. We are objectified and trained from an early age to drive toward the future to achieve and acquire more. We're told that's where the happiness lies. This only distances us from happiness. Consider the workaholic, who tells himself he'll be satisfied with the next promotion, conquest, or raise. He dreams about acquiring a bigger house, fancier car, golf membership, trophy wife.

However, should he reach these goals, he will not be satisfied because new ones immediately arise. His life will feel empty because he continues to believe that only the next acquisition or achievement can fulfill him, but it never does. Ironically, if that same hard-driving man ever discovered how to live in the moment, rather than in the past and the future, his work would likely produce even better results than his obsessive drive ever did.

Of course, when you're that man it's hard to understand.

For the 2000 season, I was that man.

I'd fallen into the trap of wanting only to reach the next goal, to become all that others expected me to be. Then, when it was obvious I wasn't having that kind of season, I avoided reality by focusing on the past, regretting every decision that had brought me to this unhappiness. (The ego lives only in the past and future, never in the present.) I'd sit in my huge home and think, "I wish I weren't making all this money. I should have never left Toronto and taken on all of this pressure." But money and pressure weren't the real causes of my depression. The trouble arose because my ego tricked me into believing that "You'll only be happy when you live up to all the expectations, just down the road . . ."

With the Jays, I'd arrived at a place within myself where I could play the games, then leave them behind to continue experiencing whatever came next in my life, the new present. Sure, a tough loss or a key error might eat at me for a while, but most of the games only lasted three hours and I was done with them. In Los Angeles, a game could last twenty-four hours, as I'd think about past mistakes and future opportunities all night long and well into the next day. I was like a nervous stock investor who is miserable when the market is down and remains uneasy even when the market is up. My obsessive need to hit home runs brought impatience into my life. I didn't enjoy time away from the park, because I was anxious to get back in the batter's box to hit balls over the fence so that I could finally rest easy. When I actually stepped up to the plate, I'd be overanxious, always in a hurry to get those missing home runs. The more impatient I got, the more focused on the future, the worse the results. I was in a rush at the plate, I was impatient in my relationship with Lindsay, I rushed into my decision to buy a big house, and I was rushed with fans who were excited to meet me. On that last day of the season coming home from San Diego, I'd even been driving like a maniac up the I-5 freeway, rushing to get home to leave the season behind!

PRESENCE

The 2000 season was over, but I wasn't in for any long hiatus from baseball after that final, disappointing game against the Padres. I'd accepted an invitation in the middle of the year to participate in a United States versus Japan All-Star series to be played in November in the land of the rising sun. I looked forward to getting away from Los Angeles with Lindsay, hoping to solidify what had become an on-again, off-again relationship the previous summer. Also, I looked forward to experiencing the Japanese style of professional baseball and their devoted fans, who'd followed American baseball for years, and whose interest in our game became almost obsessive after Hideo Nomo led a contingent of MLB All-Star caliber Japanese players to the United States in the nineties. Ordinarily, I wouldn't worry about being on top of my game for a mere exhibition series, but I couldn't help feeling that I had something to prove (the little man kept whispering to me that I'd never have been chosen for the

USA squad back in May if they'd known how disappointing the last months of my 2000 season would be).

So, in mid-October, to prepare for the series, I threw my bat, batting gloves, tee, and a bag of balls into the trunk of my car and headed to the local batting cages, which were owned by my parents, Ira and Judy (together, they ran the hitting school, with my outgoing mother working the front desk and my father giving lessons to kids). I had keys to the place and liked to sneak in before opening hours, hoping the quiet would help me to rediscover the meditative aspects of my practice. Even with the pressure of performance behind me, I still couldn't get it right. My swing still felt long and cumbersome rather than effortlessly powerful. The meditative, no-mind qualities of the work I'd savored as a Blue Jay remained out of my reach. Even at the tee, with the ball sitting idly, I couldn't get rid of my jumpy, overanxious stride, the troublesome emblem of the previous summer.

Then one day I got to the cages a little later than planned and the place had already opened.

I was going through the motions of my tee work: Place the ball on the tee, take a breath, swing, take another breath, place another ball on the tee, swing again, and so on. I couldn't find what I was looking for. My mind spun with ideas on how to make everything right. (The irony being that it was my mind's obsessive searching for pathways to stillness and presence that kept me from finding *any* stillness and presence!) After yet another disappointing swing, I stopped in disgust and looked around, hoping to break the negative cycle. Out of the corner of my eye, I caught sight of a little boy hitting off one of the token-fed pitching machines. No more than eight years old, he had a fluid swing; He stroked pitch after pitch. On his face was the most peaceful look, the expression of being utterly awake to the present moment. Absorbed in the act of hitting the balls, he only came out of his meditation when the light went off and the machine called for another token. I knew he wasn't thinking about his swing, about expectations, or about missing pitches.

He wasn't thinking about anything; he was just hitting.

After using his last token, he returned his borrowed helmet to my mother at the front desk and, after a moment, he turned toward me. Meekly, he made his way in my direction with one of my baseball cards in hand (I suspect my mom gave him one from the stack she kept at the front desk). He held out the card and a Sharpie and politely asked, "Mr. Green, would you please sign my card? I'm a huge Dodger fan."

"Of course," I said, taking the card and the pen. "I saw you hitting over there. I think you're gonna make it to the big leagues someday with that swing of yours. Can you teach me how to hit like that?"

He chuckled at my compliment, assuming I was joking.

I wasn't joking. I was hoping to regain the presence that he took for granted. As he walked away with his father, I laughed to myself. There I was, signing my baseball card for a young fan even as I was envying *his* ability to hit in presence. I brought years of knowledge with me when I came to the cage; he brought only his bat and his innocence, no aims, no worries, no goals.

So, who was the real Zen master?

This reminded me of an old Zen saying, "Before enlightenment, chop wood, carry water; after enlightenment, chop wood, carry water." The enlightened are distinguished from the rest of us not by the work they do but by the *manner in which they do their work*. (How many of us are able to become as fully engaged in our activities as is a child?) No matter how much life wisdom a person acquires, the chores of daily life remain the same. The enlightened, however, do not do their daily work as a mere means to an end: The chopping of the wood is *not* done for the purpose of building a fire, the carrying of the water is *not* done for the purpose of cooking food, because everything is done in the same state of presence, for its own sake, without goals.

That was how I used to approach my tee work.

Goals only came into the picture in 2000, when I felt the need to live up to my new identity. These goals made it impossible for me to "chop wood, carry water" during my tee work. Over the next couple of weeks as I prepared for my trip to Japan, I looked hard for the eight-year-old boy inside me, but he was still nowhere to be found.

The habit of being lost in goals and desires was not easy to break.

The USA team roster included many of the top players in the game, such as Barry Bonds, Randy Johnson, and Gary Sheffield. It came as no surprise that my good friend and hitting partner Carlos Delgado was included in the group as well. Another presence from my past was my first manager in the big leagues, Cito Gaston. Being reunited with Cito felt strange, considering that the last time I'd seen him I was far from his favorite player. Since then, I'd accomplished all he either said or implied I'd never do: steal bases, win a Gold Glove, hit well against lefties, and hit 40-plus home runs (to all fields). When I allowed my ego to focus on all that, I couldn't help feeling proud of having proven him wrong. However, after a few days in Japan those feelings dissipated.

Maybe it was the example of humility that the Japanese players demonstrated by bowing when they touched home plate after a home run.

Maybe it was the wisdom inherent in so many of the customs and values of their beautiful country.

Maybe it was the separation and space from my real life back in the states.

In any case, I began to see my past difficulties with Cito in a different light, and an unexpected sense of gratitude came over me. Those first years in Toronto I'd *needed* a push to learn the nuances of hitting. It took a trip halfway around the world for me to realize that obstacles often bring the opportunity for growth and change. Without them, we have no reason to veer from the status quo. So, I approached Cito on the field prior to a game (having avoided him at the outset). At first it was just small talk, but eventually I brought up our contentious years together.

"Cito, I wanted to let you know that even though we had our differences, I have no hard feelings."

He responded graciously. "I always wanted the best for you, Shawn. And I've been impressed with your game."

"Thanks, Cito."

And that was it. No big speeches.

Still, it meant a lot to me to have reached an amicable closure to a difficult period in my career. I could see now that Cito's old issues with me as a player hadn't been personal. In fact, if we'd crossed paths at a different juncture of my career, we probably would have gotten along well. But everything happens *as* it should and *when* it should. I began to consider my recently completed season with the Dodgers in a new light. Might there be something other than anguish for me to take from that?

On an off day, Carlos and I and others from our group took a trip to a famous Buddhist temple in Kyoto—Kiyomizu Temple, the Clear Water temple. It was a place of amazing natural beauty and inspiring architectural and cultural achievement.

"Why's your stride gotten so jumpy?" Carlos asked as we wandered among other tourists through the vast courtyard.

"Home runs," I said.

We stopped to take in a three-story pagoda, whose upswing design seemed somehow to defy gravity.

"What's that supposed to mean?" Carlos continued. "You always wanted to hit home runs."

"The Dodgers gave me a big contract," I answered. "I need to prove that I'm worth the money."

"No one's worth that much money," he said with a big smile.

We both laughed and continued our tour.

"I can't find the point in my swing that allows me to have separation and space," I explained as we approached Todoroki-mon (Reverberation Gate). "My weight always shifts onto my striding foot as soon as it lands, making the ball appear to come in faster and my swing actually move slower."

"It's about *balance*," Carlos said, taking in the wooded hills all around the temple. "I remember you used to talk to Yoda about it. What did he tell you?"

Carlos always asked the right questions.

I reflected back on my discussions with Tony Fernandez.

One day in camp in the spring of '99, prior to one of my best seasons, I asked Tony to explain his unorthodox drills. I'd often watched him balance on one foot atop a contraption that was half workout ball and half platform. (Tony was famous for having a bag of tricks filled with workout gizmos.) He'd face the mirror while balancing in his batting stance. As he practiced his swing, he'd stand on his left foot with his right knee up by his waist. He would then do sets of ten reps in which he squatted down on that left leg while, at the same time, taking an imaginary stride with his right leg as the bat moved backward in the opposite direction acting as a counterbalance, just as it moved during his regular stride. He was always careful to keep his shoulders level during these modified one-legged squats.

"I incorporated his drills into my tee work and weight lifting," I said to Carlos. "His one-legged stride squats made me feel as if my weight was forward and back at the same time, as if I was on the verge of tipping forward, even as I knew I was *never* going to tip over."

"Exactly!" Carlos jumped in. "You want to feel your energy ready to explode forward and power your swing. As soon as you transfer the weight off that back foot, your hands are released forward. Once that happens, there's no turning back—that swing is coming, all on its own!"

"Tony always told me that same thing," I said. "If you

come off your back foot too soon, then your body no longer pulls the bat through the zone with same force. Instead, your hands just drift forward toward the pitcher prematurely."

As we made our way toward the Dragon Fountain, Carlos asked the million-dollar question. "You obviously know all of this already; so what's the problem?"

That stopped me. "I guess back in Toronto, I didn't understand balance as well as I thought. Sure, I implemented Tony's drills into my workouts, into my tee drills, into my batting practice swings, and even into my on-deck swings, but I didn't truly understand what I was doing. I thought I did. But I only understood one side of balance."

"Why's that?" he asked.

"Because I didn't yet understand what it felt like to be off-balance."

Carlos nodded and smiled. "Well, after last season . . . now you do."

I looked across the courtyard and saw Lindsay coming down the steps of the west gate with one of the other players' wives. I realized that my discussion with Carlos about being off-balance could just as easily have been about the last few months of my relationship with her. This two-week trip to Japan had come at a critical time for the two of us. I hoped it would be our opportunity to dive wholeheartedly back into our relationship, with balance and presence.

"The question is how you're going to get where you want to be," Carlos said.

It sounded right. But it wasn't. I shook my head *no*. "The wording of your question isn't right," I said. "It's not about how to get there. That approach has been my problem. See,

I've been obsessed about getting somewhere else, when I should've been focused on being exactly where I was, in the present moment. No past, no future . . . I need to just get back into the flow of the present."

"The present . . ." Carlos murmured. He stopped and looked around him. The ancient temple was truly magnificent. "Yeah, the present is the place to be," he said.

"Always is, wherever, whenever."

He nodded.

"But the trick, of course, is getting there," I said. Then I caught myself. "I mean getting here, being in the here and now, whenever and wherever you are."

He grinned.

"Thanks, big brother," I said.

"No problem. I'll send you my bill!"

After two weeks, it was time to go home. The trip was more than just refreshing—it gave me the chance to close my chapter with Cito Gaston and to reunite with Carlos, whose camaraderie I'd missed far more than I realized during my first season in Los Angeles. After playing together for all eight years of my professional life (along with our friend Alex Gonzalez), it had been more disorienting than I realized to suddenly be on my own in Los Angeles. There was no way I could make comparable friendships in one season. But playing again with Carlos, even for a brief exhibition series, enabled me to rediscover the lightness with which I'd played back in Toronto, reconnecting me with aspects of baseball that had been lacking in Los Angeles.

Playing with close friends made baseball feel more like Little League, like a game.

I realized now that after moving away from friendships in Toronto my performance became my sole focus. In Los Angeles, I had a job to do, period. Where is the joy in that? Where is the spirit of the eight-year-old I'd met at the batting cages?

It's no way to approach a job. No way to approach anything!

As our bus headed to the airport and we listened to a young pitcher, Ryan Dempster, perform a two-hour stand-up comedy routine, I sat hand in hand with Lindsay. Our much-needed reprieve from our hectic life back home had done wonders for our relationship. Without ordinary distractions tugging at us, we'd been able to once again be fully present in each other's company.

After the long flight home, Lindsay and I headed to my house for some rest. She'd slept for much of the flight, whereas I had suffered the effects of bad sushi and had spent half the trip locked in the tight quarters of the lavatory.

It was good to be home.

As I lugged the bags into the house, I caught sight of a box sitting next to the front door. I checked the label. It was from Carlos. Had he been able to find the Playstation 2 that I had fruitlessly tried to track down in Japan prior to its release in the United States? The box was about that size, but when I picked it up I realized it wasn't heavy enough.

I took it inside and opened it.

Wrapped in crinkled newspaper was a little-known hitting apparatus called the Dinger. He must have had someone ship this to me from his home in Puerto Rico after our discussion in Kyoto.

I pulled the contraption out of the box.

The Dinger had been invented in the '80s by several players, including Tim Wallach and my current third-base coach, Glenn Hoffman. The device consisted of an '80s era, blue leather weightlifter's belt with a simple pulley system and a tether attached to the back. The batter would wear the belt while the tether was either held by someone standing directly behind him or was tied to the back of the cage. The pulley system enabled normal hip rotation during the swing while the tether held the batter in place. The intention of the Dinger was to prevent the hitter from lunging forward. I'd never used it before, though I'd seen Carlos use it from time to time when he was slumping. This one had a lot of mileage on it, but as the company was no longer in existence, Dingers were hard to come by.

I couldn't wait to give it a try.

The next morning, I asked my dad to meet me at the cages. He always found time to help me with my hitting, and his tutelage during my childhood had provided me with the foundation of my whole game. I put the Dinger belt around my waist and buckled it tight. Because it was made of stiff, saddlelike leather, it dug uncomfortably into my skin. My father stood behind me, holding the leash at a sufficient distance to keep it taut. Had anyone seen me, I would've resembled a dog on a walk. I placed a ball on my Tanner Tee and took a swing. At first, the belt felt too restrictive, so I asked my dad to move a couple of inches closer to ease the tension. I took another swing, then turned to my dad.

"Perfect," I said. "Stay right there."

Even during that first session, I began to feel my old swing returning. The belt gave instant feedback whenever I drifted too far forward during my stride, pulling me into place, keeping me in the present rather than lunging into the future. The Dinger was the missing ingredient in my effort to recapture stillness and presence. I realized now that my body had become addicted to the habit of jumping out to the future with my stride. Even as I attempted to rediscover the sacredness and meditative qualities in my tee work, my body wouldn't allow it. You can't find a spiritual connection if your body can't stay present!

How did the Dinger enable me to approach the problem from a different angle?

Over the past months, I had attempted to replicate '98 and '99, when my natural swing had evolved out of my meditative tee work, by turning my attention to finding still-ness at the tee. But my circumstances were different now, so the process of getting back to my optimal swing needed to be different too. This time, I wasn't going to find my swing out of stillness no matter how hard I tried.

Rather, the Dinger helped me to do the opposite, to rediscover stillness out of the process of focusing on the physical nature of my swing. The Dinger enabled me to take correct swings in a place of no-mind by physically jerking me back to my balance point whenever I drifted forward, into the future.

My swing had been fractured for several months. The Dinger served the same purpose as a cast serves for a broken bone. When I broke my thumb in the minor leagues, I needed a cast for six weeks for the injury to heal. Without the cast, my thumb would never return to normal, no matter how much I thought about it or tried to heal it. My thumb needed a cast to hold it in place, and it needed several weeks for the healing to occur. Similarly, the Dinger served to hold my balance in place, and I needed to use it for several weeks to give both my swing and my connection to the present moment the opportunity to heal.

By the time January rolled around, I was ready to remove my cast.

My balance had returned and my tee work was well on its way to becoming a joyful, sacred practice once again. When I started hitting every day off the tee without the belt it felt great! I took the swing into the coin-operated cages and hit off the pitching machines. The first couple of days, my stride was a little jumpy, so I put the belt back on. (Hitting a moving ball requires a well-timed stride and the last time I'd hit a moving pitch was in Japan, when my stride was off.) Fortunately, after a few days of hitting with the belt, I was ready to go.

The real test came in mid-January.

Every year, the Dodgers held a media day to kick off the pre-spring-training workouts at Dodger Stadium. These workouts offer players in the organization the chance to get some practice before heading off to Vero Beach. I was excited to take batting practice on the field to gauge my hard work that winter.

It felt great to throw on the uniform, the classic Dodger Blue.

On the field during our stretching routine, I caught up

with some of my teammates: Gary Sheffield, Paul Lo Duca, Eric Karros, Dave Hansen, and others. Meantime, the media snapped photos and grabbed sound bites. It was great to see the guys, including our new manager Jim Tracy. Later, third-base coach Glenn Hoffman walked out to the mound to throw to my batting group. I couldn't help but smile that one of the inventors of the Dinger was pitching the first real BP I'd taken since I'd rediscovered my swing using *his* device! Though normally my swing didn't feel great until I was well into spring training (sometimes even later), today the balls came off my bat with the same helium effect as my best days in Toronto. I launched pitches deep into the seats from the left-center gap over to the right-center gap. The guys couldn't help but notice.

Karros joked, "Don't peak too soon, Greenie."

My new manager, known by the players as "Trace," was also impressed as he leaned against the cage watching. "Hey, Greenie, let me tell you something. That swing of yours looks a lot quicker than the underwater swing you were featuring after the All-Star break last year. What have you been doing?"

I told him about my work with the Dinger.

He yelled out to Hoffman: "Hoffy, did you hear that? Greenie's been using your belt contraption. What do you think?"

Hoffy replied with his usual big smile, "I knew he was a smart guy! I was about to ask who our new player was."

After my gratifying batting session, I went inside to shower and head home before the freeways got too jammed. Waiting at my locker were reporters looking for quotes.

There wasn't the large media turnout of a regular season game, but most of the LA media outlets were represented.

One of them asked me, "Jim Tracy said your swing looks much improved over last year. What have you been working on?"

I kept it simple. "I've been working on slowing down my stride and being a little more balanced. Last year, my feet were quick and my bat was slow. This year, I'm trying to slow my feet down so my bat can speed up."

"You were launching some long home runs during BP. Have you added some muscle?" another asked.

"No. My workout routine is the same as always. I do yoga and a moderate lifting routine."

He then fired another question at me. "What kind of numbers do you expect to put up this year? What are your goals?"

This was a question most starters get asked prior to the season. It's a loaded question and plays into the ego's most distracting qualities. I recognized its relationship to all that went wrong for me the previous year in Los Angeles—setting a numerical bar, a measuring stick, to chase throughout the 162-game schedule—no thanks. I answered the question differently this time than I had a year ago. "I don't have *any* numerical goals for the coming season. I'm going to take it one at-bat at a time or, better yet, one pitch at a time. Last year, I tried too hard to fulfill statistical expectations, including my own. I'm not falling into that trap again."

The reporters weren't altogether satisfied with the answer, but it was the truth.

"I hear you used Glenn Hoffman's old batting device during the off-season?" another reporter asked.

I nodded. "The Dinger."

"How did it help you?"

I considered. "By restraining my body when I swung, it helped me to restrain my mind."

The reporters didn't follow up the question. Sportswriters are rarely interested in discussing mind/body issues.

"You sure you don't want to project a number of home runs you'll hit this season, Shawn?" somebody asked.

"I'm sure."

Heading home after the workout, I thought about the connection between the body and the spirit. I wondered why I had seen so many athletes deliver their best performances when they were injured or sick. Dodger fans remember Kirk Gibson's home run in the '88 World Series. He could barely hobble up to home plate with his injured knee, yet he hit one of the most dramatic home runs in baseball history. There were many times I saw teammates who could barely get off the training table somehow perform with greater success and grace than they did when their bodies were 100 percent. I, too, had played some of my best games with a bad back or the flu. I never understood this phenomenon. But now, I had a few ideas . . .

Often, when our bodies and lives are working perfectly, we take the present moment for granted and get lost in our minds and egos. However, when we suffer an injury or get sick, the body pulls us back by drawing our attention to our pain, which inevitably resides in the present moment. This is why in some monasteries monks are taught to raise their hands during meditation if they grow too connected to their thoughts. The master then comes over and whacks them on their backs with a stick in order to create a painful sensation, which knocks their attention away from their thoughts and back to their bodies.

Whenever awareness is placed in the body, *presence* emerges.

This is why most meditative practices focus on the body. Almost all require some type of connection to the breath. Consider the calming impact of taking a deep breath when upset or anxious. One conscious breath can relax the body, whether at bat, at the free-throw line, in the middle of a contentious business meeting, driving on the freeway, or talking through a relationship issue. One of the simplest yet most effective forms of meditation is to simply observe your own breathing, paying attention to each inhalation and exhalation. Once connected to the body, mind and ego lose their grasp and stillness emerges, but this is not common in our culture. Walk in any big city and you'll see pedestrians who are focused only on getting to where they're going rather than connecting with the action of walking or being where they actually are. It may be the forward tilt of their bodies or the focus of their eyes on their next steps that indicates the pull of the future upon them.

Usually, injuries and illnesses occur when we are lost in time and least capable of being in the moment. Perhaps injuries, illnesses, and failures are sometimes our bodies' way of telling us that it's time to refocus our attention.

This is what happened with me.

My swing had been my form of active meditation until my ego intervened, physically pulling me off balance and into the nonexistent future. Fortunately, the Dinger enabled me to hold my body where it needed to be, and everything else followed. Soon, my daily sessions of stillness with space and separation permeated other areas of my life, as they had back in Toronto. In the weeks leading up to spring training I made changes in my life. I moved back to Newport Beach, having gained sufficient separation from the ego to realize that I didn't need to be a local Los Angeles hero, but was all right being wherever I was most comfortable. And Lindsay and I worked through our issues and were better than ever.

By the time we left for Vero Beach, we did so as an engaged couple.

I headed into the season with a much deeper understanding of stillness. It had been one thing to discover it as a young, unencumbered player in Toronto, but it had been a greater challenge to rediscover it after losing it the year before in Los Angeles.

It takes discipline to remain present. Before I lost it, I took it for granted.

I embarked on the new season as a more grateful and humble person.

I'd rediscovered stillness in my swing and it felt good; nonetheless, it didn't pay immediate dividends in games. A third of the way through the season my numbers tracked below my disappointing 2000 season. In the past, I'd have panicked. But now, I kept my mind out of the equation and simply immersed myself more deeply in my daily rituals. When I was doing my tee work, I was only doing my tee work. When I was fielding ground balls during BP, I was only fielding ground balls. Even when I was putting on my jersey and spikes prior to a game, I was only putting on my jersey and spikes.

Having gone painfully wrong in 2000, I'd come to appreciate the value of maintaining complete attention throughout the day. I'd learned that true happiness doesn't come from achievement or acquisition but from losing oneself in one's actions (which inevitably serves to keep the ego under control). I maintained the same focus on each small task at the ballpark, regardless of what my statistics might say about me on any given day. In the process, tasks that used to be just work were now enjoyable.

Chop wood, carry water.

At the plate, my swing and balance were good, but my timing remained imperfect. This was something I couldn't work on at the tee or during BP, but only in actual games, because only there does the ball move at full speed. So, I had to just allow it to show up. You can't force a flower to bloom or fruit to ripen on the vine; it needs to happen when it is supposed to happen. In the meantime, I absorbed myself in my activities and remained ready. If my mind grew impatient with the process, I'd go to the cage before BP and hit to the point of exhaustion, swinging for as long as possible without stopping. Maybe fifteen minutes, maybe twenty . . . until I was dripping sweat and couldn't take another hack. It was during those last swings, when I was too exhausted to think anymore about my mechanics, that I'd lose my mind and find my way back to the present moment, where impatience for results doesn't exist.

Being fully absorbed is the key. While absorption has

never been easy to find, today's multitasking world makes it more challenging than ever. Email, Twitter, Facebook, texting, cell phones . . .

Remember, a simple definition of Zen is "doing one thing at a time."

Simple, but not easy.

Another technique I employed to overcome my mind's attempts to pull me out of the moment was to allow myself to think about a bad at-bat only as long as I kept wearing my batting gloves. When the gloves came off in the dugout, I let go of the bad at-bat. And my use of batting gloves in my spiritual practice didn't stop there.

My practice of throwing my batting gloves to kids in the stands every time I hit a home run at Dodger Stadium began as an accident in April 2000. While on deck in one of my first home games with my new team, I noticed a big tear in one of my gloves. I didn't have time to run inside and grab a new pair, so I went to the plate. Coincidentally, I hit a home run and afterwards tossed the torn gloves into the stands. The Dodgers' legendary broadcaster, Vin Scully, wondered on the air if this was something the new guy did after every home run. When I heard about Scully's comment, I thought it sounded like a good idea and soon it was something the new guy did after every home run.

By my second season in Los Angeles, the practice began to serve as more than just a fun way to connect with young fans; for me, it served as a reminder to remain connected to the present moment and detached from my ego. Just as I didn't want to dwell for long about a bad at-bat, I didn't want to allow myself to get too caught up in home runs either. The victorious jog around the bases was plenty. By throwing the heroic gloves to the stands, I notified my ego that the home run was over. Becoming attached to success is just as dangerous as becoming attached to failure.

By June of the 2001 season, my patience paid off.

We began the month with a seven-game road trip. Both Gary Sheffield and Eric Karros were hurt, and so more than the usual offensive load fell onto my shoulders. Fortunately, my hard work and presence in the cage, along with the patience that had allowed me to wait without panic for my timing to arrive, were rewarded in Houston.

We were facing Scott Elarton, a tall right-hander. In my first at-bat, with two strikes, he threw me a fastball up and away. I took an effortless swing and lofted a high pop-up that nonetheless made it into the stands of the short porch in left field (one of the shortest home runs of my career). Distance notwithstanding, I knew my timing had arrived, not because of the result, but because of the feel. My stride had landed in that ephemeral moment I thought of as "the last bit of early," and my swing suddenly had optimal separation and space.

Two days later, I had three hits: a single, a double, and a home run, this round-tripper being one of the farthest of my career, ricocheting off a rarely conquered sign twenty feet over the 435-foot mark in centerfield. By the time we completed our road trip I'd amassed five homers in seven games, which was the first time since Toronto that I'd gotten home run hot.

That week of games marked a turning point for me as a Dodger, not only because I rediscovered my timing, but also because I finally began to truly feel like a Dodger, not a Blue Jay. Working as a team in adverse circumstances (without our number three and five hitters) had evoked a sense of camaraderie as well as a sense of responsibility. I once again felt like a player my teammates could rely on. It felt great.

I was now a wiser version of the player I'd been in Toronto. Of course, I knew better than to think I had it all figured out (especially as there was nothing to figure out, at least not with the mind, since my rediscovering success at the plate had been about getting out of my head and into the moment). As a Blue Jay, my ego would jump in to take the credit for my success as if I'd done something great. Now, I knew that there wasn't any *doing* with which to credit myself; instead, there was only *allowing*. My job as a wiser hitter was just to take my swings with the proper balance, separation, space, and presence. I needed to do this as my daily, disciplined routine without any further motive or purpose. By creating this environment, I allowed it to show up. I didn't will it to show up, but allowed it. If it never showed up, I like to think that would have been okay too and I'd have kept on with the daily work regardless.

But it *did* show up and in a big way.

I played the game from a deeper place than ever before. As a result, my statistics improved and everyone loved me again. This time, however, I didn't buy into a false, egocentric sense of myself but just kept on chopping away at the tee every day (occasionally pulling out the Dinger if I felt my balance drifting forward). Pride serves as a warning that we are connecting to our egos, which we should only ever do with full awareness. This is why I paid close attention to the feelings of pride that accompanied my being the current Ironman in Major League Baseball, possessing the longest consecutive-games–played streak at 415. Though Cal Ripken's all-time Major

League record of 2,632 consecutive games played wasn't in jeopardy of being broken, I was proud of my accomplishment and status. After having fought to become an everyday player during my first three seasons under Cito, I was happy to have played in every game since Andy Petitte broke my wrist midway through the '99 season. I had never ducked tough pitchers or taken a few days off for a sore back when I was slumping at the plate, as many players do.

But on September 26, 2001, I had a decision to make.

For the first time in my career, the holiest Jewish holiday, Yom Kippur, conflicted with a game against our rivals, the Giants. I am not a very observant Jew; still, I was a notable Jewish athlete and I wore the same uniform as the great Sandy Koufax, who'd set an important precedent when he sat out a World Series game for the high holiday. I wanted to acknowledge my respect for my Jewish heritage. However, sitting out the game meant giving up my consecutive games streak as well as missing a game against a team we trailed by just two games with ten to play. And with two more home runs, I'd reach fifty for the season.

Tempting . . . but I had learned over the past few years that circumstances often provide us with clues and opportunities as we navigate our twisting paths. I knew exactly what I was going to do.

I had to let go of this streak in the same manner that I let go of my batting gloves after each home run. I needed to maintain distance from my statistics so I wouldn't fall back into my 2000 mindset, when I fruitlessly chased that one hundredth RBI and twenty-fifth home run all the way to the last at-bat of the year in San Diego. I had managed to remain present all season long and yet now that I was nearing a nice, round 50 home runs, was I going to allow my ego to take over yet again? No.

While publicly acknowledging Yom Kippur was not a strictly religious decision, it was nonetheless of enormous spiritual importance to me. I wanted to show respect for the customs of my heritage. Additionally, sitting out the game further severed connections to my ego, allowing me to let go of my label as Major League Baseball's current Ironman. In the Jewish faith, Yom Kippur is the Day of Atonement. I was grateful it came along just when it did, as my public observance furthered my pursuit of "at-one-ment," being at one with the present moment.

From a personal standpoint, the season ended well, my connection to the present new and improved. Almost incidentally, my statistics reflected all that was now right with my swing. My 49 homers surpassed Duke Snider and Gary Sheffield's all-time Dodger single-season home run record. I drove in a career high 125 runs and batted .297, the second highest average of my career.

I was a hero again with the fans and in the press. From my perspective, these numbers' real significance was that they reflected my ability to overcome the ego and to reconnect to the beauty of the present moment, the beauty of chopping wood and carrying water.

THE ZONE

I find it amusing when baseball experts extrapolate statistics for an entire season as early as May. Sure, they'll admit that spring training is too disjointed a time to evaluate where a team or player might be. And in April everything remains a blur, with half the players trying to settle into new homes in new cities and many of the games being played in adverse weather (rain, cold, and occasional snow). Further, a hitter's batting average in April can drop a hundred points just by having a bad doubleheader. But by May there are news stories about guys on pace to hit 80 home runs and 200 RBIs. Local media hit the panic button when their first-place team has a shaky first month, while the one or two last-place teams that start the season with a winning record shock and excite local fans. But players know that by the end of the season water always finds its level.

I never got off to a torrid start (except for that '99 season). Tall, lanky power hitters often start slowly, as longer arms and legs equate to longer swings that require nearly perfect timing. Lacking the brute strength of thicker power hitters, I never had the luxury of *muscling* homers. Timing was fundamental for my swing, so my hitting was often a matter of feast or famine. By late May 2002 I had experienced six weeks of intense famine (hitting .230 with just three home runs). Nonetheless, I had learned my lesson about getting caught up in results, so I remained disciplined, maintaining my chopping-wood approach to keep my attention on the present moment.

Unfortunately, my bosses and the media weren't so patient.

During a home stand in mid-May I went 0 for 9 against the Mets without hitting a ball out of the infield. Before one of those games, I happened to be standing on the field with a golf club doing a photo shoot for a magazine when *Los Angeles Times* columnist T. J. Simers arrived with a big smile on his face. He'd come to the stadium to prepare his next article, which was to be about my poor start. Simers' relentless scrutiny left many players fuming and unwilling to talk to him, but I didn't mind his criticism. I understood that his columns aimed to incite emotion both in his victims and his readers. Now, I couldn't help but laugh. There I was, standing with a golf club in my hand even as he'd come to the stadium to ask me why I was currently so horrible at swinging a bat; this scene was custom made for him.

"T. J., this article's going to be too easy for you!" I said, acknowledging the golf club.

He laughed. "Isn't that the truth! There are so many ways I can go with this." He began questioning me as I finished the photo shoot. "Are you any better at swinging a golf club than a bat?"

"Believe it or not, I actually *am* worse at golf."

"Wow, I'd have to see that to believe it," he said with a grin. "Tell me, Shawn, did you know that so far this season you have more strikeouts than hits?"

"No, I actually didn't know that, but now I do. Thanks."

This was how our interview process went over the years—a lot of sarcasm, but all in good fun (at least until I'd read his scathing articles).

"What's been your problem? Are you getting soft now that you're a newly married man?" he asked.

Lindsay and I had married the previous November. My personal life couldn't be better. "That must be it, T. J. It's all her fault!"

"When you're playing bad how come you never throw your helmet or show us that you care?" he continued. "You know I refer to you as *the puddle* due to your lack of emotion."

"Where's the competitive advantage in my getting lost in my emotions?" I answered. "The best thing I can do to help my team is to take it one at-bat at a time. Anger and rage aren't going to help me get more hits. Being focused *will* help. That's all I can do."

T. J. wrote his less than complimentary article at the end of the week and I continued with my 0-fers, going hit-less on Thursday and Friday against the visiting Expos, still unable to get a ball out of the infield. Fans who'd chanted "MVP! MVP! MVP!" when I came to bat eight months before, started booing me now whenever I made an out. I even began to hear groans after missing a pitch for strike one. The booing, T. J.'s highlighting the fact that I had more strikeouts than hits, manager Jim Tracy's frustration with my performance . . . it all began to get to me, and I felt myself shifting my attention away from chopping wood and onto the need for better results. Suddenly, I was staring down a road of trouble.

Tracy called me into his office, which was located between the clubhouse and the showers.

I took a seat.

"I think it might be best if I give you a breather tomorrow, Flaco," he said. *Flaco* means "skinny" in Spanish, and it had become my nickname during my first year with the Dodgers.

"You've been scuffling pretty bad and I think you could use a day to relax," he continued. "Show up tomorrow, throw on the uniform, and watch the game. Look, if we're going to have a chance this year, we need you for the long haul. So take a break and come back ready to get rolling."

I couldn't argue with his logic. At first glance, it might seem that one day off can do little good. But even one day without having to gear up for the intensity on the field allows a struggling player to put on his uniform with a new lightness. Sometimes, that's enough to break a negative cycle. I left Tracy's office and began my hour-long drive home at eleven o'clock that night, thinking about how to keep from falling back into the snare of the ego. As I navigated south, traversing one freeway to the next—the 110 to the 5 to the 605 to the 405 to the 73—I thought about the roadmap of my approach to hitting so far that season.

I'd navigated different drills. Over the first seven weeks of the season, I'd used the tee every day. Sometimes, I mixed in the Dinger. I tried some flips from hitting coaches Jack Clark and Manny Mota, and I took extra batting practice. I even went to the extreme of hitting right-handed in the cage in hopes that when I turned around to my natural side it would feel better by comparison. These tactics helped, but I still didn't find that elusive timing of my stride, the most delicate and enigmatic part of the swing.

Of course, it may seem that with all the experimentation, discovery, analysis, and practice I'd already devoted to hitting, I should have permanently conquered its technical aspects by now. But that wasn't so and could never be. Like every other complex activity, hitting is dynamic, which is what makes it not only a continual challenge but a great teacher. Besides, no one's body or awareness is ever 100 percent the same from one at-bat to the next; similarly, no two pitches are ever truly identical. Thus the act of hitting, like life, is always a work in progress. One must master a skill, and then master it again in a different way for new circumstances, on and on . . . Yes, sometimes it's frustrating, but it's always enlivening and ultimately beautiful.

So, it was back to work on the stride.

I knew that my front foot landing properly was my gateway to the zone. A fraction of a second late and the rest of my swing would have to rush to catch up; a fraction of a second early and my body would tense up as it waited. I reviewed the different types of strides I'd employed this season. I'd begun with a normal, traditional stride in which the foot just moves forward. Next, I changed to a Chipper Jones-style stride, which consisted of taking a small, quick step back (a mere toe tap) with my lead foot before striding forward, a sort of double-stride that got the process started sooner. That didn't help. Next, I shifted to my Albert Belle-style stride, in which I'd pick up my front foot and then put it right back down in the same place, thus landing sooner. That didn't work either. Finally, I tried my Jose Canseco-style stride, wherein I'd pick up my *back* foot about half an inch and then stomp it down immediately before striding with my front foot.

Nothing worked . . .

Was it time for my last resort?

No stride at all.

Without a stride, I'd be unable to generate much power. I recalled my former teammate Tony Fernandez, who used to sacrifice a few games by going with an ultra-heavy bat to get his swing right. He took the long view. Perhaps it was time for me to sacrifice some power over the following week in order to find my timing.

The next day at the stadium, I had my day off. On such days, a player has two choices: one is to do nothing, the other is to get to work. Both options have value. Sometimes, the best thing a person can do is enjoy separation from the cause of the stress. Other times, some extra sweat helps resolve problems. I opted for the sweaty day, excited to work on my new stride or, rather, my no-stride.

First, I did my tee work. Next, I took batting practice on the field, with no stride. Finally, I asked hitting coach Jack Clark to join me for a *long* session in the cage. We brought coach Manny Mota with us to do the throwing. I wanted to hit with no stride to the point at which I'd be physically unable to take even one more swing, pulling another old technique out of my bag of tricks: hitting to exhaustion. Of course, this approach cannot be overworked as it burns a lot of energy (and energy is more valuable than gold during a 162-game schedule). The purpose of the drill is to take the little man out of the swinging process and to reconnect with the simple, physical movement of hitting.

I grinded through the first fifteen minutes, pretending my front foot was nailed to the ground. It felt awkward. After making sure Manny wasn't going to faint from exhaustion, I asked him to throw another fifteen minutes. At last, Manny said in his heavy Dominican accent, "That looks better, Flaco, your swing's shorter and quicker without your stride."

"Thanks, Manny. But I'm not done. Are you okay to keep throwing or should I grab someone else? I don't want to kill you down here."

"Come on, Flaco. You know I can throw all day."

"Great," I answered, wiping my soaked head and neck with a towel. "Hey, I hope when I'm ninety I'm in as good shape as you are!"

He gave me a look, a smile, and then threw the next pitch behind my back.

"Okay, Manny, I'll just keep my mouth shut and swing," I said, laughing.

Over the next ten pitches, the little man finally packed his bags and *it* took over. My dog-tired swings, in conjunction with my no stride, became suddenly effortless (for the first time all season). I'd become a witness rather than a doer—line drive after line drive. I kept this up for nearly ten minutes, at which point my legs began shaking and I could barely rotate anymore.

As I took off my batting gloves, I noticed a hearty blister on my hand. I was so connected to the act of swinging that I hadn't even felt it. Now, it burned as my sweat seeped into the open wound. It felt good. Maybe the pleasure came because the blister was a badge of hard work, or maybe the pain just cemented my connection to the present moment.

Maybe this blister was the start of something good.

My work for the day was over. I took a shower before the game and changed into my uniform. Since I was going to be riding the pine, I wanted to be comfortable. I felt great having found a connection to the zone during my cage work. It didn't matter that the connection happened during practice rather than during a game. Hitting is hitting, whether you're playing wiffle ball or facing Cy Young.

I was back on track.

The next game, I went to the plate with my no-stride approach. Because my swing was quicker now, it took me a few at-bats to recalibrate my timing. By my fourth at-bat I made contact, grounding out to the first baseman. I knew I just needed to be patient (like Tony Fernandez with his heavy bat). On my last at-bat, I got the timing right and laced a ball from the Expos pitcher, my good friend Matt Herges, off the wall in right-centerfield, my first hit in nearly twenty at-bats. It felt good, even if it resulted only in a smattering of mock cheers from the crowd. After the game, we packed our bags for a road trip to Milwaukee and Arizona. I was happy for a change of scenery, anxious to put on the road-gray uniform and play for a while away from the booing. Besides, I was hopeful about my no-stride approach. I'd finally snapped my 0-for streak. Maybe my timing was coming around sooner rather than later. Maybe something good would come of it on the road trip.

The week that followed was like no other in my entire career. In some statistical ways, it was like no week any major league ballplayer had ever experienced. My swing became literally effortless, and everything came together to a degree that I never imagined possible. Psychologists call it a sustained peak experience. Ballplayers call it being in the zone or being locked in. Recalling the historic week now, I am struck by how intensely grounded I was in the moment. There was no past, no future, only the present. For that reason, the most accurate way of describing the zone may be to look back at what I was actually experiencing while in the midst of it.

Milwaukee
May 21, 2002

I'm sitting here in my hotel room waiting for my midnight room-service snack, surprised by what happened tonight at the ballpark. I continued with the no-stride approach, figuring I'd sacrifice at least a week to get my timing down and start seeing results. But it showed up tonight. I stood in the batter's box for each of my five at-bats with my at-tention focused on the image of my front foot being nailed to the ground. Only when the pitcher entered his windup did I extend my attention from that foot out to him. Wait a second . . . Sportscenter *is about to show highlights of our* game. I want to check out my stride in the two home run swings I had tonight.

Hey, my swing looks so much shorter and so much simpler!

But here's another surprise on the television.

I actually *did take a stride*, even though I intended to keep that foot locked in place. Still, the stride was smaller and more efficient than it's been all year. It's funny how, as a hitter, you have to intend to make extreme changes (such as having my foot nailed to the ground) in order to break bad habits, even though the actual differences between before and after may prove subtle, almost indistinguishable. It turns out that the intention of making a change may be as important as the actual mechanical change itself.

I've experienced this during yoga sessions where I'll move into different poses as my off-season instructor Steve guides my awareness: "Move your attention into your fingers, feel your whole hand on the floor. Now, feel your body lengthening through your shoulders. Imagine that your 'sit bones' are extending away from your heels." He guides my awareness continuously during the workouts. When I first began, I was amazed that simply by imagining my rear end, or what Steve called "sit bones," moving away from my heels, I could feel a deeper stretch in my hamstrings.

I guess that's no different than transforming life habits. The body and mind resist change. It takes not only time and repetition, but also often requires extreme intentions (such as my imagining my foot being nailed to the batter's box) to achieve even subtle results. I notice this phenomenon in many areas of my life: working out, meditation, diet.

Speaking of eating . . .

Dave Roberts and I ate today at my lucky Italian

restaurant, Giovanni's, which I've been going to since my rookie year with the Jays. Last year, I went there every day of our three-game series in Milwaukee and I homered in each game. I told Dave the place had lots of homers in their chicken parm. And tonight he hit his first homer of the year! I guess we'll be going back there again tomorrow.

Seeing Sarge today also gave me a boost. I haven't seen him since we were in Toronto together back in '99. The Brewers are lucky to have him as their hitting coach. He rode me pretty hard on the field during batting practice, as he always loved to do. He joked with me, "Greenie, I've been watching your swing on television and it looks pa-thetic!" I told him I was getting my timing under control and that I'll always be one step ahead of him. He laughed. I'm sure my two home runs tonight will shut him up for the rest of the series. He's always been a big supporter, always a boost to my confidence.

Glad I stuck to my plan . . .

Okay, it's late and I'm tired. I hope Lindsay calls back soon so I can go to sleep. I'm anxious to hear about her doctor's appointment. Six weeks pregnant! Things happen when they're supposed to happen. We may try to control and change the flow of life to fit into our own schedules, but life moves at its own pace. All we can do is chop wood each day, and make adjustments as needed, and remain nonresistant to life.

Phone's ringing . . . a good end to a good day.

It takes discipline to keep your eyes on process rather than on results. After all, resisting immediate failure is a natural enough impulse; however, doing so often means that you also unintentionally resist the potential for greater success.

My disappointing first season in Los Angeles had taught me to fight for only one thing each day, remaining in the present moment. As long as I remained present, I'd be prepared when it arrived, the flow of life, the entry to the zone. That first game of the Milwaukee series, I recognized the emergence of it taking over my swing. That game was the start of something great, for which I needed only to discipline myself to remain present and let the flow of life take me for a ride.

Midair
May 23, 2002

I'm on the plane now heading from Milwaukee to Phoenix and I'm exhausted. It's safe to say that my inkling that I might be entering the zone after hitting two home runs on Tuesday night was an understatement. The next night against one of the best young pitchers in the game, Ben Sheets, I hit a triple and scored the only run of our 1-0 victory. Even though I struck out twice, I felt great at the plate (it is possible to have good at-bats that end in strikeouts).

I woke up this morning feeling physically tired but unusually alert and aware after last night's game. I didn't make it back to Giovanni's for lunch today, because I had to get to the ballpark at nine for the one o'clock start. I guess Giovanni's isn't the source of the magic. Otherwise, all that happened for me at the plate today wouldn't have happened.

Superstitions are fun, but they don't explain success. Still, baseball players are famously superstitious, probably because superstition seems to offer a way to control those things that are actually out of our control, such as finding the zone. The truth is that even the most skilled hitter can't dictate when the zone will arrive or how long it will stay. The common anxiety attached to that lack of control explains why so many of us, myself included, naively choose to believe that if we repeat all that we were doing as we entered the zone we'll manage to hang onto it. In baseball, teammates and coaches harp, "Don't change a thing!" So, streaking ballplayers eat the same meals in the same restaurants, leave for the stadium at the exact same hour, and try to do everything else in the same manner as before.

If only it were so easy.

The only real way to exercise any control of the zone is to simply be prepared for its arrival. I learned that if I followed my routine with complete presence, chopping wood and carrying water each day without worrying about the past or the future, the zone would show up. Yes, sometimes I needed to tweak my swing. But, after that, the best thing to do was to absorb myself in my daily routines. Unlike superstition, a routine is an exercise of discipline, creating a space through which the zone can enter of its own volition. When we practice our daily chores without ulterior motives, a routine becomes like the rubbing together of two sticks; if you keep at it fire eventually happens. You don't know exactly when it will arrive—it just does.

And, when the zone arrives, daily routine becomes critical to sustaining it. Nothing yanks you out of it faster than the little man jumping on your shoulder to whisper, "Wow, isn't this wonderful! Let's think about how great we're feeling at the plate and how we've finally got it all figured out." The best way to guard against that little man is to rely on your daily routine, done with presence. Achieving the state of no-mind is the key to getting into the zone and sustaining that state is key to staying there for as long as possible.

Back to the journal entry from May 23, written when I was traveling at 38,000 feet high, both literally and figuratively.

. . . I poured every cell of my body into today's game. Six-for-six for first time in my life (including Little League), with four of the hits being home runs! I've repeatedly recapped today's game with the media and my teammates, so I may as well put it here too. I'll write about it and then it'll be over. Just as I use my batting gloves for closure after both home runs and strikeouts, I'll use the completion of this journal entry as my symbol for closure. Today's game is over and I have a new game tomorrow.

My first at-bat was against Glendon Rusch, a veteran left-handed pitcher who is aggressive with his fastball while also mixing in some breaking stuff. With a runner on second and a 0-2 count, I took a fastball high for ball one. The high fastball was intended to set me up for the next pitch, which I suddenly knew would be a breaking ball over the plate that would start at that same height but break downward into the strike zone. He was hoping I'd be fooled and take strike three. I wasn't fooled. I hit the pitch just inside the line past the first baseman for an RBI double.

In the second inning, with runners at first and second and two outs, Rusch threw a breaking ball for a strike (a smart pitcher will often start you off with the same pitch you pounded for a hit on your previous at-bat, betting that most hitters will mistakenly think he's scared to throw the same pitch). Next, he threw a hard fastball inside for a ball. Immersed in the moment and with my awareness completely directed out to the mound, I knew what he was going to throw next even before he did.

He was going to come inside on the next pitch.

While I got into my stance, I imagined a pitch coming on the inside corner to make sure my eyes would be ready for it when it happened. Next, I placed my attention on my front foot being nailed to the dirt and then moved my attention out to Rusch as he came set. He threw a fastball on the inside corner and I hit a high fly over the wall in right field for a three-run homer. (It's so nice to be hitting the ball with backspin again! Those high pop-ups carry for an eternity when my swing is right.)

By the time my third at-bat rolled around, I was locked in. I led off the fourth inning against a rookie I'd never faced before, Brian Mallette. He threw me a 1-1 slider on the inner half of the plate and I put it over the fence and onto the walkway in right-center field. I didn't even feel my legs moving as I jogged around the bases. When I faced him again in the fifth inning, I no longer needed to focus my attention on my right foot being nailed to the ground.

Everything was working now on its own.

His first pitch was up and away for a ball. Somehow, I knew what was coming next: a two-seam fastball away. I wasn't thinking about it with my mind, no guessing. He wasn't tipping his pitches. I just knew. This sense of knowing came from a place much deeper than the mind. I was almost out of my body. At that moment, there wasn't a pitch near the plate that I couldn't handle. When the pitch came, I launched it deep into the seats in left field. I floated around the bases with blissful ambivalence, fully occupied as the watcher rather than my usual role as the doer. Of course, I was happy to have just hit my third homer of the day (and fifth in three days), but I was residing in a place beyond numbers.

Fully engaged in the now, without the slightest feeling of anxiety or judgment about what was taking place, I led off the eighth inning against another new pitcher, Jose Cabrera. Sure, I wanted to hit a fourth home run, but I didn't change my approach. He threw a 1-0 fastball down, maybe even below the strike zone, and I lined it right back up the middle for a single. Even though it wasn't a home run, it may have been the hardest ball I hit all day.

When I got back to the dugout, five for five, manager Jim Tracy said to me in his Southern accent, "All right, Flaco, take it on in and shower up. We've seen enough of your act today!" It's always nice to leave a blowout game early, but I told him I'd rather finish this one. In the top of the ninth, Adrian Beltre hit a two-out homer to bring me to the plate for a sixth at-bat. The opposing crowd welcomed me with cheers. As the game was already a blowout, I think almost everyone on the field and in the stadium (except Jose Cabrera, out on the mound) wanted to see me hit a fourth home run.

I walked up to the plate. I couldn't help wondering if Cabrera was going to put a ninety-plus miles per hour pitch into my rib cage. I wasn't worried (God knows every part of *my body has tasted leather over the years), but just curious. Plenty of teams would send such a message for the next time they faced me (which is next week in Los Angeles). I dug into the box and realized that the little man was giving it one more try to distract me. My attention had been so focused today that maybe he thought my exhaustion had weakened me. It almost worked. I stepped out of the box, took a breath, and said to myself, "There's no sense thinking now." I shifted my attention back into my body and then onto the guy on the mound, dissolving the little man.*

I took the first pitch for a ball. The next pitch was a changeup that I missed for strike one. Then he threw a fastball down and in and I unloaded on it, my farthest homer of the day, deep into right-center field. This time around the bases, I couldn't help but smile. Today was a once in a lifetime experience, so I allowed myself to relish it. Six for six with four home runs. As I rounded third and was jogging toward home plate (and the Brewers' dugout), I made eye contact with Sarge. I think he was trying as hard as I was to hold back a smile. The look on his face said, "Are you kidding me?" He'd been with me for two of my best years in Toronto, so he knew all of the wood chopping that had created this special moment. As I crossed home plate, Sarge gave me his signature salute. It felt good. I then made my way into the sea of high-fives in our dugout as the crowd showed their appreciation with a standing ovation.

I was physically spent.

Nothing feels better than exhaustion after a full day absorbed in the moment.

Now, as I sit on the plane to Phoenix, just a few hours

removed from hitting that fourth home run, I still feel the in-tense alertness that carried me through the day. I'm beat, but I've never felt more alive.

Finishing up this journal marks the end of today's historic game. When I move back a few rows to where the guys are anxious for me to join their card game, I will have officially let go of patting myself on the back. My ego would love to live in this day forever, but the truth is it's over. All that matters is right now, sitting here on the plane.

I'm going to wake up in the morning, head to the ballpark, and face Curt Schilling and the defending world-champion Diamondbacks. My four-homer game won't help me tomorrow. The only thing that will help me is to play with the same presence that I played with today.

Arizona
May 25, 2002

Two days since my big game and not much has changed. I'm in a different city playing against a better team but that hasn't mattered. The first pitch yesterday from Curt Schilling, one of the best pitchers in the game, I lined over the wall in right field. That homer represented my seventh consecutive hit, five of which were home runs. I struck out swinging my second time up, and then stroked two more singles, going three for four in the game and nine for my last ten.

Tonight, I faced Rick Helling, a pitcher who has historically given me trouble. No matter, my hot hitting continued. He throws a cut fastball, which is my least favorite pitch. But when you're in the zone, you're in the zone. I walked my first at-bat. (They're finally realizing they shouldn't give me too many pitches to hit in certain situations.) I grounded out my second time up and then launched a three-run homer the next at-bat. For my fourth at-bat, I just missed a home run as I hit a very high fly ball to right field, scoring Dave Roberts for the sacrifice fly. Then, against lefty Eddie Oropesa, I hit a two-run homer to left-center field, finishing the night at two for three with six RBIs and two more homers.

What was amazing about that last home run was that I broke my bat. I've had a handful of broken-bat home runs during my career, but never 400 feet to the opposite field. It's too bad that my best piece of lumber is now out of commission, but what a great bat it was! Over the last three games, that piece of wood helped me go eleven for thirteen with seven home runs and fourteen RBIs. And that's not including two home runs in the first game in Milwaukee on Tuesday and a triple Wednesday. All in all, I've hit nine home runs in the last five games after hitting just three home runs during the first forty-plus games of the entire season! It's safe to say this bat died a hero. As much as I'd like to keep it for myself, I promised the Hall of Fame that I'd send it to them once I was done with it (after Thursday's game in Milwaukee, they came calling). Now that it's got a little crack on the handle it's off to the Hall.

Now, it seems to me that saving the bat would merely have served as a way for my ego to hold on to that day forever. One of my favorite quotes from *Zen in the Art of Archery* by Eugene Herrigel occurs after the master honors his pupil's years of training by giving him his best bow. The pupil is humbled. But the master warns him of the ego's desire to become attached to the bow and its representation of accomplishments and advises that ". . . when you have passed beyond it, do not lay it up in remembrance! Destroy it, so that nothing remains but a heap of ashes."

The truth is that while I was in the zone, I moved beyond the whole competition aspect of hitting. Absorbed in the act, it no longer mattered to me what team I was playing against or who was on the mound. There was only this: The ball came at me in slow motion, and I hit it. As the pitcher released the ball there was no me, no him, no bat, and no ball. All nouns were gone, leaving only one verb: *to hit.*

In such circumstances, I almost wanted to laugh as pitchers stood 60 feet, 6 inches away from me shaking off signs, full of self-importance and purpose, thinking they could get into my head by making me guess what pitch they were about to throw. How could they get into my head if I wasn't in it myself? In my more compassionate moments, I felt like calling timeout and running to the mound to tell them not to waste their time and energy trying to strategize about what to throw next because it wasn't going to matter!

In sports, if one player is competing and the other has transcended competition, who's going to win? The answer is obvious. A lot of people talk about the best players being those who compete best. They talk about players whose minds are toughest. They reason that whoever wants it more will win. Yes, there's a time and a place for this mentality, but it was never what I was after (I relied on it only when I was off my game). What I preferred was to be effortless. Meditation and presence during my daily routines aided me in this. Still, I was never in control of the zone. Rather, it passed through me as it pleased. I was only its vehicle. Top athletes play a different game than others. They have a knack for being in the zone, whether they can explain it or not. These athletes are fun to watch, not just because of their ability to win but because of the grace and presence of their actions. That week in 2002, I was one of them.

Los Angeles
May 27, 2002

I'm home after six days on the road.

I finished up the last game of the trip with a couple more singles. Today, I put on my white home uniform for the first time in a week. The last time I wore this jersey I was immersed in a horrific start to the season. The fans were booing me and I was beginning to grow impatient. The little man was threatening to get my attention.

Six days later, everything's changed.

Now, I'm among the league leaders in home runs and RBIs, and everyone loves me. My crazy successes on the field last week have swept away the negativity that surrounded my start to the season. With critics no longer breathing down my neck, it's easier to chop wood and carry water. But just as failure evokes the little man, success can do the same.

In today's game, my first back at Dodger Stadium, I fell out of the zone. I got caught up in the emotions of returning home after my historic week. I felt resentment every time I received loud ovations from the crowd, for these were the same fans who had booed me last week. I went up to the plate with too much of the I'll-show-you attitude rather than with the purposeless presence with which I'd stepped up to the plate throughout the road trip. The little man wanted me to continue my tear at home, for all to see and worship. So my stride was jumpy as I tried to hit the ball a mile. Last week, I wasn't trying at all; I was just hitting, but today it was gone. Nonetheless, I managed to topspin a solo home run on my last at-bat against Jose Cabrera, the same guy who gave up my fourth home run of the historic game last week in Milwaukee. As I rounded the bases to a standing ovation, I cynically considered foregoing my ritual of tossing my gloves into the stands. My ego wanted to communicate to the fans that they'd hurt my feelings last week with their booing. But hanging onto resentment is no way to go, so why start now? As I headed into the dugout, I tossed the gloves up to one of the younger fans above our dugout (I like to target the smaller, less aggressive kids).

Still, today was a slip-up. My awareness became connected to the emotions and desires associated with playing in front of the home crowd and my connection to the zone slipped away. But the zone isn't absolute black or white, there are shadings, and I'm still in a good place. I'll let today serve as a reminder that I need to be vigilant and disciplined with my daily routines and try to apply complete attention to every action. That's the only way I can keep the door open for it to enter once again.

• • •

Over the last four months of the 2002 season, I continued my streaky ways. For the most part, I retained my discipline of chopping wood each day and kept my attention away from results. I was like the surfer who patiently sits on his board, immersed in the present moment. Out of nowhere, a big set would roll in and an intense ride commence. After a while, the big waves would disappear and it'd be time to sit again.

My "big waves" coincided with the months on the calendar. After a small slump upon returning from my historic road trip, I regained my presence through my daily work and another huge "set" rolled in. During June, I hit twelve more home runs and had twenty-four RBIs. Included in that month was a stretch in which I homered over four consecutive at-bats against the Angels (my last two at-bats one game and then my first two at-bats of the next). During July, I was back to sitting on my board waiting for the waves to return. The following two months finished up my seesaw year with a productive August and a hungry September. Now, I realize that my epic stretches were actually by-products of my bad stretches. The reason I had ten- and twelve-homer months was that I was willing to accept the three- and four-homer months. By not tweaking my approach every time *it* disappeared, I enabled *it* to eventually reappear.

The zone isn't something that can be controlled. It is a force of nature—a force of the universe. It shows up when it shows up, and it comes packaged in an infinite number of ways. A great afternoon at the beach with friends, a belly laugh with your kids, and a deep conversation are all examples of it showing up. You can try to plan these moments or try to recreate them at a later date, but they can rarely be controlled or anticipated. Still, we live for moments like these. In the end, all you can really do to ensure them is absorb yourself fully in every moment and be patient. By doing so, the Zone will arrive more frequently in your life, work, and activities than ever before.

NONATTACHMENT

Unfortunately, the following season, 2003, featured little time spent in the zone. Instead, it offered the greatest physical challenge I faced in my career. Life is always a work in progress and just about the time you think you've got it all figured out . . . During the last month of the '03 season, *Los Angeles Times* beat writer Jason Reid broke a story about something I'd been hiding, that I'd been playing all year with an injury. I hadn't wanted to make excuses for having only 12 home runs and 61 RBIs at a late stage of the season, but my closest friend on the team, Dave Roberts, grew frustrated with the harsh criticism directed at me in the media and so, after much prodding by Reid, he'd told him about my injury. Now, seven of us from the organization were crammed into the tiny training room office, some sitting on a beat-up couch that had likely been part of the Dodger organization for as long as Tommy Lasorda, while others crumpled in office chairs or leaned on the cluttered desks.

"I called this meeting so we can all be on the same page

today when the media asks about Shawn's injured shoulder," said Dan Evans, the team's general manager.

I knew the front office didn't want to expose itself to further criticism for having failed to shore up our hitting. Everyone knew we had the best pitching in the league and the worst offense; for this reason, the L.A. papers had been hammering me for failing to perform up to expectations. After all, I was the guy making lots of money to hit home runs. The fans' frustration peaked in early July during a Saturday game against the Arizona Diamondbacks. Our pitcher Odalis Perez took a no-hitter into the eighth inning at Dodger Stadium and like every other defender I was on my toes, willing to do whatever I could to keep the no-hitter intact. Shea Hillenbrand of the Diamondbacks hit a low line drive between me and the right field line. I charged, ready to dive, but the ball was well beyond my reach. Sure, I still could have uselessly dived for show to please the fans (demonstrating what Mel Queen used to call "false hustle"), but then if the ball got past me our eighth inning 2–0 lead would have been placed in serious jeopardy. It was a clean base hit, nothing more, nothing less. Nonetheless, the stadium erupted in boos, all directed at me. I knew that only a small portion of the fans' disapproval was actually related to my not having dived. Most of it was about my subpar hitting that season.

Believe me, if you want to experience terrible solitude try standing alone in right field with forty thousand people targeting their negativity at you. Of course, verbal abuse from fans in the bleachers is part of the job for all outfielders, but I'd rarely been booed in the field by my home crowd and never with such uniform ferocity. That July day at Dodger

Stadium it seemed an entire city was enraged by my disappointing performance that season. Of course, they didn't know that in my efforts to be a selfless, egoless player, I had kept a shoulder injury a secret, at least until now.

The meeting in the trainer's office continued.

"How are we going to handle it when the media asks if the shoulder injury is the reason for Shawn's struggles this year?" the general manager asked.

I jumped in. "Look, I don't want to make excuses. Remember, I didn't reveal this to the media. Obviously, the injury affects my swing. But if a player's healthy enough to be in the lineup, then he's healthy enough to produce. No excuses."

The meeting concluded with the team's legendary orthopedic surgeon Frank Jobe laying out the medical details of my recent MRI. He spoke with a deep, authoritative voice. "Shawn can continue for the remainder of the year, though he has fraying of the labrum, which we're likely going to have to clean up with surgery after the season."

As the room emptied, I asked Dr. Jobe if he had a minute. He was a great man and always very accommodating to the players. He shut the door and said, "Sure, Shawn. What can I do for you?"

"What exactly is going on in my shoulder?"

"In simple terms, it's gotten chewed up, or frayed. It's like you have a bunch of tiny, stabbing hangnails in there."

"It's always sore," I said. "But it bites me especially hard on high pitches and pitches I hit out in front of the plate, like changeups. Still, I don't remember any particular moment when I hurt it."

"Sometimes a player hurts himself on a specific swing or

throw. Other times, the injury occurs as a result of years of overuse and repetition. All those swings you take every day in the cage have finally caught up to you, Shawn."

The first image that popped into my head was my prized possession—the batting tee. "Are you saying that this injury is the result of the extra work I've done with my batting tee over the years?"

He nodded. "It doesn't matter if the ball is moving or sitting on the tee. This comes from the thousands of swings you've taken and the torque you've placed on that labrum."

I thought of the drill in which I put the tee up to its highest point, level with my armpits. And I recalled the drill in which I put the tee far out in front of home plate and then would reach as far as I could with my right arm to hit an imagined pitch back up the middle. Lately, those swings had evoked the most pain. But these drills were the root of my practice . . .

After Dr. Jobe left, I stayed in the office, alone.

Was my extensive and dedicated tee work, the staple of my career actually the *cause* of my injury? The tee had transported me from a solid major-league player into one of the game's most productive hitters over the last five seasons. And more, the tee had transformed my whole life! Those daily fifteen- to twenty-minute sessions were my meditation. There, I'd learned to separate my awareness from my mind and move it into my body and ultimately into the present moment. There, I first began to understand what it means to chop wood and carry water. The tee was a good thing, right? So, how could you overdo a good thing? Was this disillusionment?

Or was the tee presenting me with yet another impor- tant lesson?

Sitting on that old couch behind the closed door, I dove deeper and asked myself a hard question.

Why had I really chosen to keep the injury to myself?

One reason was that if I was going to play, I didn't want the competition to change the way they pitched to me because of my injury. That not only would have affected my at-bats, but also would have altered the strategic way other teams pitched to the guys directly before and after me in the lineup. A second reason was that I believed the pain would go away on its own. In the past, I'd felt less intense pain in the same shoulder for days at a time before it would indeed disappear (as an everyday player, you rarely feel 100 percent, but learn to work through aches and pains). However, the most important reason I kept the injury to myself was that I had privately regarded the pain as an opportunity to destroy my own ego.

During my time in Los Angeles, I'd experienced the give and take between staying in the moment and getting caught up in the ego. Each time I thought I had it figured out, the little man would come up with a new way to wedge himself between me and the present moment. And each time I'd eventually find my way back again by chopping wood during my daily routines. But as I struggled through the first half of the 2003 season, I came to believe that the more pain I endured the more my ego might be diminished. I thought suffering would bring me what I was looking for.

That's not how it worked.

Instead, I'd grown resentful. I began to feel superior to players who pulled themselves out of the lineup due to minor injuries. I took pride in the fact that I'd never gone on the disabled list, not even when Andy Pettite broke that bone in my wrist with a fastball back in '99. Plenty of players get sore backs when they're coming up against a Randy Johnson–quality pitcher or when they're swinging poorly. I never did that. And so I came to believe I was better than those other players because I thought I didn't have an ego big enough to concern itself with things like slumps or ducking pitchers.

But wait . . . I thought I was better than others?

Isn't that ego, too?

It suddenly became clear to me. Over the past few years, I'd succumbed to an image of myself as an antisuperstar. I'd always been self-consciously careful to suppress my emotions during the great times and to unapologetically face the music during the bad times. I'd shunned many opportunities for endorsements and increased fame that being a sports star in Los Angeles offered. I'd taken pride in showing up to spring training much thinner than other power hitters, many of whom were later revealed to be steroid users, because I knew that my relative lightness highlighted the fact that I still could hit the ball farther than almost all of them. Sitting by myself in that training room office, it finally dawned on me: I was just as caught up in the *image* of myself as a humble, antisuperstar as other players were caught up in their images of themselves as traditional superstars!

How could I not have seen this?

I had chosen to tolerate the disillusionment of management, the media, and fans, rather than simply to acknowledge my shoulder injury because I had believed that a tolerance for painful criticism illustrated the conquering of my ego's need to be a top hitter in baseball. What I didn't realize, however, was that by doing these things I was actually feeding a new identity that my ego had chosen for me, that of the enlightened, spiritually superior athlete. By publicly saying, "Don't look at me," I was in effect saying, "Look at me!" Cultivating a feeling of spiritual superiority to my steroid-juiced, tabloid-seeking colleagues, I was, in a subtler way, as fully engaged in the ego as they were. I lost touch with *presence* as surely as if I had dressed in a gold suit and paid to have my face on a billboard on Sunset Boulevard.

Once again, how tricky the ego is!

And so just as overdoing my tee work damaged my shoulder, my self-conscious attempts to combat my ego had been overdone to the point of actually creating a whole new persona (a pure exercise in ego!). My subsequent attachment to this image was no different from the player who wants to be known as the greatest of all time. Both images are mere fantasies that promise a happier and more fulfilling future, denying the precedence of the present moment. Sure, some might suggest that my aims were somehow inherently more admirable than the guy who's after mere fame and a truck-load of money, but I disagree, as both I and the stereotypically driven athlete were looking to *become* something rather than simply to *be*.

Life isn't about continually getting to the next level. Too many of us view life as if it were a school in which we constantly are trying to graduate to the next grade. In 2000, I'd fallen into the ego's trap of, "you need to be the hero," and now that I'd injured my shoulder, I'd fallen into the ego's new trap of being the unappreciated antisuperstar.

The fight is never ending.

Was my immoderate labeling of the ego as an evil enemy where I'd gone wrong? After all, the problem is not the ego itself, which is almost impossible to permanently quash, but getting lost in the ego and falsely identifying it as one's own true essence. Might simply being aware of the ego and watching it from a place of separation and space be enough to keep oneself present?

I realized now that I'd doubtless get lost in the ego again—many times—but that as long as I was able to wake up to the present moment I'd always find my way back. Just recognizing the ego for what it is means that you're not completely lost in it.

Maybe injuring my shoulder wasn't such a bad thing after all, as it exposed me to the idea that becoming too attached to anything, even good things like my tee work and spiritual seeking, creates problems. Overdoing the tee work had torn my shoulder, and my self-conscious attempts to become egoless had served only to make my ego stronger than ever! Both missteps were the result of becoming *too attached*. The previous year when I was most intensely present in the zone, I hadn't felt attached to anything but had been simply present. All sense of myself was lost in the action and so there was no separation between me, the doer, and the doing. The experience was beautiful because of this unity, which is the way of our universe. When Eastern philosophies teach of the importance of nonattachment, I believe this is what they are teaching: the way of the frayed shoulder.

I left the training room after about twenty minutes alone.

There was such an ironic duality in my tee work. Even years ago, during my best stretches as an up-and-coming star with Toronto, my daily tee work was quietly chewing up my shoulder. All those good swings had not only made my success a certainty, but also my future failures. This realization helped me to understand a quote from *Siddhartha*, by Hermann Hesse, "The world itself, being in and around us, is never one-sided . . . never is a man wholly a saint or a sinner."

Shortly thereafter, I allowed Dr. Jobe to give me a cortisone shot for the first time in my career. If I needed his prescription to help ease the pain of my shoulder down the stretch run (provided it wasn't going to cause further damage), then I'd do it. If the team fell out of contention over the next couple of weeks and doctors wanted me to get surgery before the season ended then I'd do that as well. I was done fighting my ego's fight, done trying to prove something by enduring pain.

Within a couple of days, the shot took effect and my pain was much relieved and much of my power returned. In the remaining twenty-four games of the season, I had twenty-three RBIs and seven homers and ended the season with a .280 average, 19 home runs, 85 RBIs, and a league-leading 49 doubles. While those numbers were a far cry from the 40-plus homers I'd hit in each of the previous two years, this season was among the most significant of my career, not because of numbers, but because it had exposed to me yet another layer of my ego—a layer that I likely would never have noticed without the injury—and taught me that the more I self-consciously resisted its pull, the more I became attached to the suspect identity that formed in the resistance. I learned *acceptance* of what is.

A place of no judgment, no goals . . . the place where actual life happens.

And that is a much better place to be.

Within weeks of the completion of the season, I went in for the only surgery of my career. Drs. Ralph Gambardella and Frank Jobe performed the work and all went as planned. Doctors told me I should be ready to go for spring training 2004. However, I would have to change my off-season workouts. I could no longer practice yoga, and I would have to forsake much of the upper-body lifting that I normally did. I wouldn't start swinging a bat until January, and that would be done under the supervision of the team's training staff. My focus that winter was different than it had been for every other winter of my career. Rather than working to get into top shape, I spent my time just getting healthy.

I played through spring training and into the first couple months of the regular season with my shoulder less than fully healed. The rotator cuff around the labrum was stronger than ever (thanks to the Jobe exercises that I performed on a daily basis), and I was free of the smarting pain I'd experienced on each swing in 2003. But now I felt the duller pain of an injury that's on the mend. And that wasn't the only complication to the first months of the 2004 season—I'd agreed to moving from the outfield to first base if it meant the team might acquire a strong new bat.

For the previous fourteen seasons, I'd *only* played in the outfield. In spring training I worked only part-time on the new position, as it was uncertain if the move would actually occur. Unfortunately, it wasn't until the day before our first regular game of the season that I learned I was actually going to be playing first base.

The move was no small thing (particularly on such short notice)!

The game is so much faster standing 100 feet from the batter as opposed to 275 feet away in the outfield. Playing in the outfield was second nature to me. I knew where to play all the hitters and where to throw the ball in any possible situation. I didn't need to use my mind at all. But, as a new first baseman, I had to remind myself to do even the most elementary things, such as to run to the bag to take a throw. Before every play, thoughts swirled in my head: "Okay, on a hit to either center or right field, I'm the relay man on the throw to the plate . . . on a bunt, I'm charging . . . on a ball in the gap I'm the trailer to the relay man . . ." Suddenly, I was forced to think my way through the games, at least when I was playing defense.

Analyzing and thinking is stressful, but I had no choice. And complicating matters was that during those first few weeks of the season I was frankly scared to death playing so close to left-handed power hitters. And even the glove was different! I'd used the same outfield glove for the past eight years and it had become like an extension of my hand. The leather was patched, but I'd never found another glove with such a perfect pocket. And now I was using a new first base-man's glove that was only partially broken in.

Thirty minutes before every game, my palms would get sweaty as I envisioned playing the new position. I felt like an actor trying to learn his lines before going on stage every night. Naturally, I tried to separate my stressful defensive situation from my batting, but it was impossible to avoid the mental exhaustion that accompanied all that intense and anxious thinking.

And so my offensive struggles of '03 continued through the first half of the '04 season. Nonetheless, I did the best I could, though I wasn't going to habitually keep my mouth shut anymore about the challenges, clinging to the illusion that my being silent made me better than other, more ego-motivated athletes. My shoulder still bothered me, sore from the healing process. Time was the only thing that could make it pain-free. As my workouts had been limited in the spring, my strength was compromised. Also, I'd had to limit my cage work. I could still hit off the tee, but I took only about half the swings I once had. Struggling at the plate, I'd have loved to perform my drill of hitting to exhaustion, but that would have done further damage to my shoulder. All I could do was dig in and battle through the difficult, early months of the season.

At least now I allowed myself to express my emotions. If I was angry, then I would be present in my anger. If I was anxious playing first base with Barry Bonds just ninety feet away at the plate, then I would be present in that tension. If I was excited after getting a big hit or after our team won a close game, then I would fully experience the emotion. I was finished trying to live up to an image of who I *wanted* to be or who I *thought* I was. It is all too easy for any of us to get lost in such manufactured images. Often, the perceptions and expectations of those around us strengthen the weighty images of ourselves we already carry around. Habitually, we label ourselves and others, and before long these labels create a false sense of identity that we spend far too much of our energy trying to justify. Sometimes we habitually identify ourselves with our jobs, our possessions, our goals; other times we habitually identify ourselves with our problems, our frustrations, our illnesses, our weaknesses.

Better to just be where you are, to just feel what you feel.

In early June I headed back to the place where my big league journey began—the SkyDome in Toronto. This was the first time I'd gone back to play a regular season game there. Walking into the stadium, I felt like an alum going back to see his former school; everything looked both exactly the same and entirely different. Many, from among the security guards to the ushers to the clubhouse staff to the fans to the handful of players with whom I'd played as a Blue Jay, brought back memories. One of the first things I did was grab my tee and head to the cage—the place where the seeds of my maturity had been planted years before.

I walked into that cage with a different perspective than that with which I'd entered it before. Eastern philosophy proposes that you can never step into the same stream twice. I was no longer a player on the rise, full of swagger. Now, I was trying to recover from both a frayed labrum in the shoulder and a frayed ego, both products of having pushed positive work ethics to immoderate levels. I sat on an old foldout chair in the cage, smiling as I noticed a Tanner Tee sitting at home plate. I recalled my battles here for independence with Willie and Cito as they'd tried to change me into a pull hitter. I recalled the soulful meditations I'd experienced here as I grew into a power hitter. I re-experienced the joy I'd felt here with the Sarge and all my close friends on the old team.

As I stood and set my Tanner Tee up and put the bucket of balls on top of its base for extra support, my eyes welled up. I was glad that no one else was in there—my teammates would have thought I was nuts. I hit for an extended length of time, making an exception to my new set of rules for the tee work.

Afterward, I headed into the clubhouse invigorated.

Still, my slow start continued fostering doubt and harsh criticism from media and disapproving fans; worse, it resulted in my being bounced around the batting order. As a Dodger, I'd always batted third or fourth, but now Jim Tracy began moving me all over the lineup. He said he wanted to help me find my groove. But moving in the order merely brought *more* attention to my struggle, resulting in yet another mini news conference at my locker.

Throughout this turmoil, I avoided getting too caught up in surface waves by no longer clinging to the misperception that I had to be the antisuperstar or enlightened ballplayer; I could be more forgiving of myself. And expressing my emotions in these difficult times helped. I still didn't throw equipment after a strikeout or yell at prodding reporters, but neither did I suppress my feelings. In the process, my emotions ran through me quickly as I watched them from a place of presence, and then they were gone.

On the first of July in a home game against the Giants, my hitting at last came together. In my final two at-bats of the closing game of the series, I hit a home run and a game-winning double. More important, I'd found my swing, which had been missing since 2002.

It had been a challenging fifteen months. And the challenges were not over.

In the previous nine years, I'd had only one game that conflicted with Yom Kippur. In 2001, I sat out that game and broke my consecutive games streak. Now, in the heat of the 2004 pennant race, the league had scheduled not one but two games on Yom Kippur (which spans sundown to sundown). With a slim lead over the Giants, we'd be playing a Friday night game followed by a Saturday day game; clearly, the most crucial series of the season. I was swinging a hot bat, and so the media pressed hard to learn how I was going to handle the situation. My eventual decision provoked much debate on talk shows and in articles. I would play the Friday night game and sit out the Saturday game. The middle path. Some people felt this was the worst possible solution, demanding that I either stand for one thing or stand for the other. But I had moved past my ego's need to do the right thing in the eyes of the world. Instead, I did what was most consistent with what *I* felt was right, which was to acknowledge the holiday to show my respect for my Jewish heritage and, at the same time, to be there for my team and the Dodger fans as we strived to reach the playoffs. In the Friday night game I hit a two-run homer in a 3–2 win, which proved crucial in a pennant race that went down to the second to last game of the season. It felt good to hit that homer, but it felt even better to make a decision that was aligned with my heart rather than with my ego.

We won the team's first division title since 1995. My second half—on par with my very best seasons—went virtually unnoticed by the Dodger world, as my struggles at the plate the previous year-and-a-half had tarnished my status as one of the top power hitters in the game. Fully healthy, I had regained my form. But if a tree falls in the forest and no one is there to hear it . . .

Even more frustrating was that the Dodger front office wasn't focused on team chemistry. By the July 31 trade deadline, the new ownership's recently appointed General Manager, Paul DePodesta, traded away much of our team, despite our three-game lead in the National League West Division. He dealt fan favorite and All-Star catcher Paul Lo Duca, who was not only a key player on the field but also a team leader. Two-thirds of our starting outfield, Juan Encarnacion, and my closest friend on the team, Dave Roberts, were also sent packing. Our bullpen had been our team's greatest strength, but this didn't keep veteran relief pitchers Tom Martin and Guillermo Mota from being shipped out during the crazy, two-day whirlwind. No one in the baseball world could believe that a first-place team would make such drastic moves midseason. All the players were taken by surprise, having expected that we'd merely add a key player or two, as contending teams typically do at the trade deadline.

The playoffs came and went for us very quickly.

We played the best team in the National League, the St. Louis Cardinals, and lost the series three games to one. Even so, that playoff week was a highlight of my career, as it was my first opportunity to play in the postseason. We lost the first two games in St. Louis before returning to Los Angeles to play in front of the home crowd. As I started around the bases after hitting my second home run of game three (which we won 4–0 behind the pitching of Jose Lima), I allowed myself to be fully present in my emotions, giving the only fist pump of my career as I rounded first base. I could feel the elation of the Dodger fans, who hadn't much approved of my play since 2002. Somehow, the cheers of the fans seemed to express a more personal tone that day, as if they were saying to me, "We're cheering you now for more than what you've done in this one game." Did they sense that I would never again circle the bases in a Dodger uniform? Maybe I sensed the same thing (we players all suspected that the new regime planned to overhaul the organization). But, here and now, I'd given the fans a reason to love me again, which was actually all they really ever wanted to do. Sure, they had an image of who I was *supposed* to be, just as for years I had carried around such an image. And whenever there was a gap between what they thought I was supposed to be and what I was, they felt frustration. Well, I'd been there too. Who was I to judge them?

And I was still learning all about frustration.

During the 2004 season, I'd felt frustrated when management and media seemed unreasonably impatient with my recovery from the surgery. It seemed as if everyone expected me to be 100 percent the day I put my uniform back on. The truth was that it was bound to take time for me not only to strengthen my shoulder and get through some lingering aches and pains, but also to repair a few bad habits in my swing that I'd developed while playing hurt. Additionally, I felt frustrated when I was bounced around the lineup, even as I was trying to find consistency in my game. I felt frustrated when our first-place team was dismantled at the midseason trading deadline. I knew that these frustrations had arisen out of my own preconceptions that were based more on how I thought the world *should* be than on how it actually was. Yes, I'd grown more adept at refraining from trying to live up to an idealistic image of how I should be, but I still held to concepts of how the world should be. An imperfect spiritual perspective, yes, but I'd learned to no longer deny my imperfections at the cost of expressing my true feelings. And so, for better or worse, there was a lot about the 2004 season that fell short of my expectations about Dodgerland; one thing about allowing yourself to acknowledge your emotions as they arise: Sometimes, it hurts.

At a low point, I sat in the car of my agent, Jeff Moorad, in the parking lot of Dodger Stadium. He was leaving the agent business to become an owner. I confided to him that I had grown so frustrated with the baseball world that I was contemplating retirement. He advised against it strongly; but having opened myself up to my own feelings, I couldn't deny the pain. Walking away from all of it seemed to promise relief, though it saddened me to think that my baseball journey might conclude at a place of negativity.

After the season, new owner Frank McCourt asked to schedule a meeting. I knew he'd ask me if I'd be willing to waive the no-trade clause in my contract. Management already had traded away much of the heart of the team and I knew they were unlikely to re-sign Adrian Beltre, a close friend who'd just completed the greatest season of any teammate I ever played with, batting .334 with 48 home runs and 121 RBIs. He carried us to the division title. But the team was being led by a young general manager whose mind was crowded with theories and ambitions, focused on building his *own* team and making his mark, rather than by a seasoned baseball executive's patience and wisdom. Our division championship team, which had taken several years to build, was being dismantled. I'd always wanted to finish my career in my hometown, but I knew it was time for me to move on.

Or perhaps time to call it quits. I didn't know.

Was my frustration turning to such bitterness that I could actually leave a game I still loved?

Baseball and bitterness . . .

The combination made me think of my old idol, Ted Williams, who'd died less than three months before. Ted had played for years through his bitterness, never once even tipping his cap to his hometown crowd. But is that any way to be? I wondered whether Ted would do it all over again in the same manner if he were given another chance. I'd met him a couple of times, but those times I hadn't really known what to ask him. Now, I wished I could speak to him again.

The night before my meeting with McCourt I had a dream, which I recall as follows.

Q & A WITH TED WILLIAMS ASKING ME QUESTIONS

TW: You think you know something about bitterness, kid? You feel the organization has let you and your teammates down, right? You feel the media and the fans misunderstand what you've been struggling through the last couple of years, right?

SG: It's not just the organization or the media or the fans . . .

TW: It's you, too?

SG: Yeah, I have to admit that despite everything I've worked so hard to grasp these last few years . . . you know, about the ego. Well, I still wish I'd got more done out there. But the front office . . .

TW: (interrupting) I know, Shawn. You're frustrated with championships squandered, roster changes, overbearing media coverage, incompetent ownership, management, this team or that team.

SG: Exactly, Ted.

TW: Tell me what any of that's actually got to do with baseball.

SG: (silence)

TW: Tell me, Shawn, why did a whole stadium of kids want to play catch with you all those years ago in Seattle? You weren't yet an All-Star. You hadn't ever hit twenty home runs in a season, let alone forty. No Gold Glove. No Silver Slugger. That was all in your future.

SG: They wanted to play catch with me just because I was a big league ballplayer.

TW: That's right. And it's a damn good reason. Hasn't everything you've been seeking to learn these past years taught you this much? It's all just a game. All of it! But it's a damn beautiful one. And it's all about *playing.*

SG: Yeah, and what could be better than playing the game, right?

TW: Let's not get carried away, Shawn. There's one thing that's better.

SG: What?

TW: Playing the game while also being a Marine Corps fighter pilot in World War II and the last man to hit .400.

SG: Okay, I can't argue with that. But then, not everybody can be Ted Williams.

TW: That's right, kid. And not everybody has to be Ted Williams because I got that covered.

SG: So, I don't have to be Ted Williams . . .

TW: Of course not. Isn't that already settled by now? How many times are you going to regress on all that business of what you're supposed to be? It's simple. You just have to be yourself, whatever the hell that is at any given moment.

SG: So, if you had it to do all over?

TW: Yeah, my bitterness may have been the only real mistake I ever made in the majors. Who knows? It's too late for me, now. But as for you . . . Relax, kid. Just open your eyes and take it all in.

· · ·

At the conclusion of my meeting with McCourt, I agreed to let the Dodgers trade me to the Arizona Diamondbacks, where I resolved to make another fresh start. This time I'd play the game with my eyes wide open, simply appreciating all the beauty that the game of baseball (and the bigger game of existence) might throw my way.

Not a bad prospect.

• • •

By the midpoint of my first spring training with the Diamondbacks, I was already well adjusted to my new teammates and surroundings. The transition to the first new team
you play for is the most difficult; after that, it's just a matter of
different faces in the locker room and different uniforms on
the field. I enjoyed my morning drives to the training facility in Tucson. There's nothing like the beauty of the desert
sky just after sunrise; it was the highlight of early trips to the
office in the Cactus League. Still, I couldn't help wondering
how I'd feel about the desert by the end of summer. I suspected the heat would be even more challenging for Lindsay
than for me, as I'd be spending most of my time under the
roof of Bank One Ballpark in Phoenix, while she'd not only
have to keep our two-and-a-half-year-old daughter Presley
occupied in 115 degree heat, but would also be very pregnant with our second daughter, due in late August.

Arriving each morning by eight at the facility, I'd wave
to the security guard at the players' parking lot and to the
smattering of fans along the fence with their binders of cards
and Sharpies. I always signed for the new kids, but just waved
to the adult regulars, the ones we saw day after day and year
after year. It didn't bother me if they sold my autographs on
eBay, but I didn't feel the same obligation to stop for them.
They were always around: at the hotels, waiting by the players' parking lots, hanging over the dugout. Some players
found them annoying. But I saw them differently. They loved
baseball, even if they were profiting from our autographs.
They promoted us and the game. In the end, fans are at least
as important a part of our national pastime as are any of the
players.

And among the fans there was one who stood out.

Her name was Susan, and she was legendary in Arizona for her simple and undemanding dedication. I'd noticed her even when I was a visiting player. Middle-aged and pleasant, she never missed a game or workout. She arrived at the stadium before any of the players and welcomed us all with individualized shoutouts. During batting practice, she'd stand over the dugout and watch every swing intensely. She required nothing from players but an occasional hello, and, even though a few of the guys didn't even bother with that, she still supported us all every day. She was a warm-hearted woman who filled a void in her life with baseball. We all have voids in our lives. What makes the world interesting and fun are the often eccentric and always diverse ways we fill those voids. What a beautiful tapestry this makes of life.

I'd wave to Susan and finish signing autographs before walking through the clubhouse door. As I looked at the different lockers, I'd be reminded how the players in this camp, and every big league camp, also made up a tapestry of diverse strands. Every team consists of players of different nationalities who speak numerous languages, players of different races from every possible economic background, players in their late thirties with growing families who are putting the finishing touches on their long careers, players who are not yet old enough to buy a beer, pranksters, and quiet, reserved guys. Of the sixty or so players at any spring training camp, many never get to the Major Leagues. Others hang on for a few years and only get a taste of their dreams. Few ever actually experience the wealth and fame that those on the outside assume is the norm for those on the inside. Still, in the clubhouse, differences between players weren't the most important thing. What always mattered most was that we wore the same uniform and played the same game.

Where my teammates were five years ago was as irrelevant as where they'd be five years from now. What mattered was that we were teammates in the present. True, the outcomes of spring exhibition games are usually regarded as insignificant—people come just to see ballplayers they know play a game they love to watch—and yet, whatever these games lack in competitive intensity, they more than make up for in simple playfulness. In fact, it may be that fans and players connect more deeply to the pure joy and beauty of baseball in a setting like this, where results don't matter so much.

Spring training ballparks aren't crowded and dominated by message boards and Jumbotrons. Instead, they're designed for fans to relax in the sun and experience a game without the frills and constant marketing and entertainment-oriented distractions of the big stadiums. Spring training takes us all back several decades, to a time when the empty spaces between the pitches and the swings of the bat were just as important as the pitching and hitting itself, where the space between the actions is just as beautiful as the action itself.

As the regular season began in Phoenix, I came to appreciate the mornings not only because of their coolness, but also because morning was when I got to be with my family. Unlike most folks who look forward to evening because that's when they return home from work and get to toss the ball around in the backyard with their kids, the opposite was true for me.

My working day usually began in the afternoon. Only in the late mornings did I get to play with my daughter Presley and hang out with Lindsay, whose life was about to become more complicated than ever with the coming birth of our second daughter in August. She had her hands full, enabling me to be at the stadium.

The lifestyle of a major-league baseball wife offers the comforts that come with money and fame, but it also brings particular challenges. Lindsay and I learned that no matter how idyllic a situation may seem, there are always difficulties. Such is life. I feel a sad empathy for anyone whose life is driven to extremes because he or she falsely believes that by becoming rich and famous problems will miraculously vanish. Happiness is not a mere byproduct of success or acquisition. Fortunately, Lindsay and I were both content before we achieved material success, so we remained content after our lifestyle changed, but I saw colleagues every day who were miserable before they signed big deals and who remained just as miserable (if not more so) after they got the big bucks. Media and marketing campaigns insist that you'll be happy when you make it big. But they're selling a fallacy, the promise of a better future, when in reality the opposite is true: contentment arises only out of engagement in the *present moment*. And even though I loved my mornings with Lindsay and Presley, my present moment always eventually involved getting packed up to go to work at the ballpark.

The competition side of my job, the actual ball games, was never my favorite part. Competition fuels the ego, which insists that we always be better than others; it's the part of us that's *never* satisfied and yet is revered, not only in sports but in business and politics. Top athletes get kudos for being fierce competitors. Yet, when I looked at the most accomplished players in sports, I rarely saw wise, happy people. Instead, I more often saw insecure and miserable egos. I watched players come up to the big leagues filled with a joy and zest for life and, then, as they became superstars, turn grouchy and resentful, lost in their numbers and how they were measuring up to other players. I didn't blame them. After all, I'd battled with the ego myself during those years in Los Angeles. But now in Arizona that battle was over for me, not because I'd achieved enlightenment or transcended the ego, but because I'd chosen to no longer fight it. The best approach to the game of baseball is just to *play* it; the same is true of life. The most fulfilled people are the ones who are always playing, the ones who don't take life too seriously. I always enjoyed my interactions with the guys—cards, games, shooting the bull, practical jokes—but with the Dodgers, I'd been too busy being the highly burdened superstar to fully engage. Now, I felt free to join in the fun. And this Diamondbacks team was an interesting group of guys, consisting as it did of either fresh-faced rookies or long-time veterans.

The Diamondbacks' Luis Gonzalez was a superstar who always maintained a playful attitude and was a positive influence on all of us. Once, he parked relief pitcher Mike Koplove's car on the warning track of the field before batting practice. Koppy had to race into the clubhouse to retrieve his keys to move his car before it was peppered with batted balls (and every batter was aiming for it). A couple months later, I got revenge for Koppy by changing some of the settings on Gonzo's new laptop so that we could take control of his mouse while he was on it. For a few days, every time he got on his computer after BP, we'd go to iTunes and buy Britney Spears' and other teeny-boppers' albums. He'd call me over to his locker to help him, and someone else would man the mouse from my computer. The joke ended when he almost bought a new laptop and had the I.T. expert at the stadium ready to shut down all of the ports because a hacker was taking over the ballpark.

We veterans, along with coaches such as Mike Aldrete and Jay Bell, had great baseball conversations while on flights, in the clubhouse, and in the weight room. That's not unusual on Major League teams. What made *this* team unique in my experience, was how often these conversations evolved into mentoring sessions for our rookies. There was such a range of experience between us that it was almost as if the veterans were serving as both players and coaches. It seemed to me as if only yesterday I was learning in Toronto from veterans Paul Molitor, John Olerud, Roberto Alomar, Ed Sprague, Joe Carter, and Pat Hentgen, and here I was now teaching a new generation.

Still, as much as I enjoyed my role as mentor to the younger players and colleague to the other veterans, my favorite part of my day at the office remained my time at the tee. There, I still honed my swing and found peace and stillness. I didn't hit with the incessant drive that had frayed my shoulder. Instead, I took half as many swings, then spent the remaining time either joking around with the guys or sharing some of my experiences with the next generation. I approached the game with the same appreciative and playful mentality that I felt when I sprayed little Presley with the hose as she laughed and ran around the yard. My life had never been richer. The city of Phoenix, named for a mythological bird that rose to a new life from the ashes of what came before, proved to be just the right setting for me, just the right place for a kind of rebirth.

Fourteen months later, in August 2006, I found myself sitting in the passenger seat while my new teammate and old friend, Carlos Delgado, drove us through the afternoon traffic on the crowded streets of Manhattan. Just two days before I'd been a member of the Diamondbacks, and now I was the newest player on the New York Mets, the best team in the National League. When the D-Backs' new owner Jeff Moorad (formerly my agent) asked me if I'd waive my partial no-trade clause to move east, I agreed. With the D-Backs out of contention, there was little point in keeping veterans around, better to get the young guys up and give them experience. Meantime, contenders always want another reliable bat for the stretch drive. And so here I was, sitting in the car next to my big brother, Carlos, with whom I'd spent the first eight years of my career, first in A-Ball in Dunedin, Florida, then Double-A in Knoxville, then Triple-A in Syracuse, then the majors in Toronto, and finally even barnstorming in Japan. And now, in New York, I'd be finishing my career with him.

Beautiful.

My move from Los Angeles to Arizona had been a big step out of the spotlight, furthering my efforts to regulate my ego. Being a D-Back had afforded me the chance to once again perceive the game with lightness, rather than as a weighty burden. By the time the Mets called, I felt sufficiently recharged to jump back into the fire. Besides, the prospect of playing for a World Series–caliber team doesn't come along very often. And I was emotionally and spiritually ready to play in New York, the baseball capital of the world. The five years I'd spent in Los Angeles battling my ego and my identity as a ballplayer had made me aware of the pitfalls of losing myself in expectations. I was ready now not only to handle the big city chaos and intensity but to enjoy it. And best of all, I was getting to do it alongside familiar faces.

Carlos wasn't my only former teammate on this team. Utility man Chris Woodward had also been a teammate of ours with the Blue Jays. Former Dodger teammates included Paul Lo Duca, Guillermo Mota, and Duaner Sanchez. Orlando Hernandez, aka El Duque, had been my teammate during the first half of the season in Arizona. In all, a quarter of the team consisted of guys I'd played with before. Familiar faces make change easier. Also, I was looking forward to playing with the game's oldest player, and one of its wisest hitters, Julio Franco. Perhaps he'd pass along some of the knowledge he'd shared over the years with Tony Fernandez.

Carlos and I drove from the FDR Drive to the Triboro Bridge. Meantime, Carlos described both the layout of the route to Queens and the layout of the Mets organization. He liked playing here (both he and the team were having great seasons). He'd never before been to the postseason, having spent most of his career looking up at the Yankees and Red Sox in the AL East. I'd only been to the playoffs the one time with the Dodgers. We both knew how rare an opportunity it was to be on a team capable of winning a World Series, and we were both grateful to be there.

"Don't worry about a thing, Greenie," Carlos said in his big-brotherly way. "I'll take you under my wing just like I did when you first signed."

"Yeah, yeah, I know. . . . I was pretty green back then." Even though I hadn't seen Carlos much in the past six years, I could still finish his sentences, from feeble puns to deeper thoughts. We were brothers.

"That seems like yesterday," Carlos said.

I couldn't believe how fast everything was moving. Presley would be four in a few months and little Chandler's first birthday was just days away. Now, as Carlos and I headed to the stadium, Lindsay was prowling Manhattan looking for an apartment before heading back to California to gather up the kids. What a whirlwind!

"And do you remember when I helped you figure out your laundry and cooked you *arroz con pollo*?" Carlos continued. "Back then, you were a skinny kid who could barely hit the ball out of the infield. Now, you're a skinny kid who's hit over forty homers in a few different seasons. I, on the other hand, was born with 'pop' in my bat! By the way, home run derby starts today in batting practice. I could use some good dinners. Are you ready, little man?"

Always with the trash talk . . .

I'd shortened my swing while in Arizona, going back to the line-drive-over-the-shortstop approach, when I got the sense that I needed to hit for average rather than for power to stay in the lineup. "Give me a week to start thinking like a home run hitter again," I answered.

"No problem. I'll even help you get your home run swing back before we start, but then it's game on. And I don't want to hear any excuses."

That's how it is with good friends, years may pass and yet connections remain strong. Friendships transcend time and space. Being at home refers to a lot more than just being in an old, familiar place. When Carlos and I arrived at the far side of the bridge, it seemed to me just like I was home again.

A few weeks later in Florida, before a game against the Marlins, I was heading back to the clubhouse with tee in hand when I saw a familiar figure walking toward me. He was wearing slacks and a golf shirt, but I recognized him immediately; years before, we'd worn the same uniform in Toronto. It was Tony Fernandez, Yoda, my old friend and mentor.

"Tony!" I called out.

He turned and his mouth unfolded into a humble smile. "Greenie, it's good to see you. How do you like playing in New York?"

"I love it. It's fun being on a good team in front of such intense fans. You know how it is." Tony had played on both New York teams. "What brings you out to the stadium?"

"I came by to see my old friends: you, Carlos, Julio. Hey, I've watched some games on television and I think I can help you out a bit, Greenie. You've been too jumpy at the plate."

"That sounds great, Tony! I'll let Downer know I'm going to be with you in the cage during BP." Rick Down was our hitting coach. He and I got along great because, unlike a lot of coaches, he had no jealous need to be the *only* one to help his hitters. If Tony had advice that helped me, no one would be happier than Downer. He understood that every hitter was different, so he'd grown adept at listening to what players need. (Many authority figures are great at talking, opining, and giving directions, but are incompetent when it comes to truly hearing others. Often, their minds are so preoccupied formulating responses that they don't actually listen to what's being said. Whereas talking to a good listener—one who absorbs every word and refrains from cutting you off with his or her own words—is a great experience.)

"Go to it!" Downer said enthusiastically when I told him about Tony.

As the team shuffled out of the clubhouse for stretching and BP, I headed to the cage with Tony and my tee. We'd had a few sessions like this during our time together with the Blue Jays. He'd shared his balance drills with me in the weight room during spring training and had worked with me in the cage to teach me to place my awareness on the inside part of my back foot. Now, he placed each ball on the tee for me and discussed his observations. Sometimes he used words to convey his points; other times, he grabbed my bat and demonstrated his suggestions, since some things are better shown than explained. Even in his street clothes, five years after playing his last game in the big leagues, his movements were graceful and effortless. I still couldn't tell if he was swinging the bat or if the bat was swinging itself.

We continued working in the cage until it was time for me to change into my game jersey. Tony reminded me to *feel* the inside part of my back foot as I started my swing, then to move the attention into my legs as my entire body sunk slightly downward with my turn. He told me I had to be more aware of my legs if I wanted to engage with the ground below me, which is where the power comes from. I thanked him and headed into the clubhouse to prepare for the game. I was dripping sweat, but it felt great. He said to call anytime I want to talk about hitting.

I'd been a professional player for fifteen years and yet I was still learning and growing as a hitter. I knew that were I to play the game for another fifteen years, like my forty-eight-year-old teammate, Julio Franco, I'd *still* have plenty to learn. That's one of the things that I love about baseball, one of the things that I love about life: there is no end to the learning. Or teaching. I hoped that someday I'd show up at a stadium or a Little League field and have the same positive impact on a younger person that Tony always had on me. As significant as his hitting advice was, it was his desire to help, his display of friendship, which meant the most.

The highlight of the 2006 season occurred at Dodger Stadium, where I drifted into foul territory in right field to get under a pop fly hit by Dodger infielder Ramon Martinez for the final out of my new team's three-game sweep of my old team in the first round of the playoffs! How fitting that the final out of our series was about to land in my glove, the glove of a former Dodger. Of course, the final out could also fittingly have landed in our catcher's glove, Paul Lo Duca, who'd spent more years in the Dodgers' organization than I had. Along with Guillermo Mota, another former Dodger, we three had been resoundingly booed that night whenever our names were announced. Why do fans boo former players, especially ones that were traded? When the new leather of the ball met the old, crusty leather of my glove, I squeezed it tightly and raised it triumphantly toward the sky.

Third out, game over!

In the infield, Lo Duca was jumping up and down with what I recognized as an exultant feeling of redemption. In the meantime, Carlos embraced the Mets' two rising stars, David Wright and Jose Reyes, enjoying the first postseason experience of his illustrious career. To me, it didn't seem so long ago that Carlos and I were the up-and-coming stars with the Blue Jays. Now, I was nearing retirement and Carlos was an established, veteran superstar. As with all things, baseball changes fast. It's futile to try to hold onto the past. One moment, I was celebrating my first division championship as a Dodger and now, two years later, I was celebrating a championship *against* the Dodgers. I watched my current teammate, Tom Glavine, running out to the mound (where all of us exultant Mets were headed) and I couldn't help but reflect that his teammate for a decade in Atlanta, today's starting pitcher for Los Angeles, Greg Maddux, was at that moment solemnly packing up his locker after the loss. Together, they'd celebrated countless victories, including the '95 World Series championship, but now they were on opposite sides. This was a lesson on the futility of trying to hang on to past circumstances, to hang on to time. In truth, there is only ever the beauty of each moment.

Oh, my ego loved beating the team that traded me—that's human.

No sense denying it.

But I knew that the truest reaction to this scene was just to be fully present to its intensity. In celebratory moments such as this it's not difficult. Surely, all of us Mets were fully present. The individual dramas and concerns that normally occupied each person's head were absent. Nobody was dwelling on a bad call by the umpire, nobody was fretting over an argument with his girlfriend, and nobody was replaying the home run he hit last inning. Individuals were forgotten and we were all lost in the moment of victory, lost in *presence*, which is where all the joy comes from. For this brief time that our goal had been achieved, there was no more *future* or *past*. But when the dust settled, the next goal would appear: to win the NL championship and by doing so get to the World Series. And so it goes, on and on. The joy of this moment would dissipate and longing would return.

But I wasn't going to worry about that trap, I was content with where I was rather than where I was heading. After a few minutes of hugging and jumping around the infield, I got pulled aside to do postgame interviews. With two doubles and a single against my former team, the announcers dubbed me player of the game. I went through a brief media song and dance, then headed into the clubhouse to shoot champagne on my teammates.

Hey, winning can be lots of fun.

But it's not always the same.

The first time I'd participated in a victory celebration was '93. I was a twenty-year-old September call-up of the Blue Jays team that would go on to win its second consecutive World Series. When the team clinched the Eastern Division in old County Stadium in Milwaukee, I felt out of place, having only been on the team for a week. During that celebration, I hung in the background with Carlos and a couple of other Double-A teammates who'd been called up with me. As I hadn't even set foot on the field of a Major League game and knew I wasn't going to be on the playoff roster, I couldn't have felt more like an outsider.

The second celebration was in '04 as a Dodger. We had a two-game lead over the Giants with two games left to play against them at Dodger Stadium. Losing 3–0 in the bottom of the ninth, we miraculously tied the game, then won it on a Steve Finley grand slam. It could hardly have been more dramatic. When Finley launched the ball deep into right field, the entire stadium erupted; we were all jumping around like Little Leaguers, completely absorbed in the moment.

My third big league taste of champagne had occurred at Shea Stadium just a few weeks earlier, when we clinched the NL East. The race had been over by the time I got traded here in late August, but it took a couple of weeks for us to clinch. Since I was the new guy on the team, I felt a little distant from the celebrating. Don't get me wrong; I had a great time. The truth is I found the greatest pleasure in watching Carlos' joy as he reached the playoffs for the first time and in seeing Lindsay and our two girls, Presley and Chandler, come onto the field to celebrate among the screaming fans. Lindsay loved watching the Mets fans go crazy (she can watch people all day). Presley was a shy three-year-old, so she kept her head buried in my armpit. She couldn't wait to get home to some peace and quiet, being a lot like her dad in that regard. It felt great to comfort her within my embrace. And Chandler *loved* being the center of attention. She'd only begun walking that week and was excited to show off her new skill. She waddled alongside the stands, relishing the fans' encouragement. She could only make it about ten yards before falling, but she loved every second of it. Too bad my kids won't remember that experience. I'll never forget it.

Now, as I sprayed champagne on the guys in the visitors' clubhouse at Dodger Stadium, I felt much more a part of the team and thus more a part of the celebration. I'd played a key role in our victory tonight, so I felt like a contributor. Another perk was that our manager Willie Randolph had agreed to let me stay home with my family an extra day before flying back to New York. Having swept the series, we had a few days off before the next challenge. And time spent with my family was more precious to me than ever.

About a week after the celebration in Los Angeles, I found myself sitting alone in the third-base dugout of the new Busch Stadium enjoying the sound of raindrops on the cement roof above my head, the sight of thousands of tiny splashes on the field, and the smell and feel of moisture in the air. I thought about a Zen-like quote from the film *Bull Durham*, "Sometimes you win, sometimes you lose, and sometimes it rains." Game five against the St. Louis Cardinals had been cancelled due to the downpour. The series was tied at two games, so plenty of people were disappointed to have to wait another day. But I wasn't. At that moment, I couldn't have been happier. Sure, I was as excited about the series as anyone else, but just then I was occupied enjoying the rain.

Being a ballplayer had taught me a special appreciation

for rain. Early in my career, I enjoyed rainouts and rain delays because the wet weather meant either a night off or an extra hour or two of playing cards. The competitive intensity and focus that goes into preparing for a game shuts off when the tarps roll onto the field and a wave of lightness transforms the atmosphere of the clubhouse to one of playfulness and relaxation. With game five's cancellation, most of my teammates were showering to head back to the hotel, carefree. In a few minutes I would too, but for a moment I enjoyed being the only player out on the bench. Sitting here, I watched lots of people doing their jobs.

The grounds crew continued its busy evening. Every so often, they'd run out and pull the tarp off to clear some of the water. Meantime, the TV camera operators cleaned their gear and double-checked that their cameras were well-protected from the rain. Still photographers snapped shots of the covered field and of players and fans. Being a professional myself, I couldn't help but admire the expertise of others. We players get most of the credit, but there are many talented professionals who contribute to the entertainment value of sports. Many of them love what they do, and the love shines through in their work. I was proud to count myself as one of them. I grabbed my bat and headed back into the clubhouse, looking forward to eating some good food, talking baseball with my teammates, then heading back to my room for a good night's sleep—an evening off courtesy of Mother Nature.

Sadly for us, the Cardinals knocked us out a few days later in game seven at Shea Stadium, denying us a place in the World Series. What a disappointment, but as a professional I understood that losing is part of the game.

• • •

Late on an August evening, ten months after we'd been elimi-
nated from the previous season's playoffs by the Cardinals, we
Mets loaded onto an airport-bound bus outside PNC Park in
Pittsburgh. After a well-played game, the peacefulness of sitting on the bus as my teammates climbed aboard was always
one of my favorite things about baseball. I rarely felt more in
tune with my body. At that time of the '07 season, we were
holding to first place again in the NL East. I'd had a couple of
hits in that night's win, had run the bases hard, and had had
plenty of action in the field, so I felt my body humming as I
settled on the bus. I felt with particular acuity the scrape on
my knee throbbing under the bandage (I'd slid into second
base and reopened a scab). The strawberry had burned sharply
in the shower; still, I was happy for the scrape because I in-
curred its ilk only by getting on base in the first place. Besides,
the mild pain kept me present and connected to my body.

My veteran status in the game allowed me two seats to
myself, three rows from the front of the bus. It's an unwritten
rule in the majors that younger players sit toward the back
and get only one seat. Though I had thirteen years of big-
league service time, quite a few guys on this veteran Mets
team had even more: Tom Glavine, Aaron Sele, Billy Wagner,
Moises Alou, Pedro Martinez, Damion Easley, and Jose Valen-
tin. Still, I sat in the third row, passenger's side, almost every
time. We're creatures of habit. The front row usually belongs
to the team leader and guy with the highest status in the
game. In our case, that was Tom Glavine. (How could anyone
argue with that?) I enjoyed being close to the front primarily
because it meant I could plop into my seat sooner than later.

And having two seats helped me stretch my legs, which often cramped up after a game. On this night, I smiled ironically to myself from my privileged position on the bus, recalling a not-so-privileged meeting I'd had just a few days before with our manager, Willie Randolph.

He'd called me into his office to discuss my playing time.

"Greenie, we're going to be giving more starts to [Lastings] Milledge over the remaining portion of the season," he said. "We need to see what the young guy can do. But don't get me wrong. You're a great asset to this team, so you'll still get plenty of action."

I flashed back to the meetings I'd had in Cito's office more than a decade before. In those days, it had been explained to me that I was losing playing time so that more experienced guys could play. Now, with the Mets in a pennant race, they wanted to conduct a sort of tryout for a younger, inexperienced guy. Because of economics, the entire game was shifting toward youth. Previously, the game had favored veterans, from crusty old scouts and GMs on down to the players, but, by the late nineties, many executives were barely out of college and the whole mindset was shifting toward youth. Fortunately, I knew better now than to resist change, which is one of life's constants

As a young player in Toronto, I had responded to frustrations with anger and pride, completely absorbed in my ego. I'd fought to prove Cito and his staff wrong, driven to succeed. That drive had led me to grab the batting tee and set off on my own way and it had been the right thing to do at that time. Maybe that's why youth and pride so often go hand in hand; we need that push at that time to send us off to create our "personal legends," as described by Paulo Coehlo in his wonderful novel, *The Alchemist*.

Now, things felt different. I'd already lived the baseball portion of my personal legend. I'd had a colorful career as a major leaguer, one that, at this point, could end or could continue. It was up to me. I was only thirty-four years old and had a lot left in the tank. Surely, I loved baseball, but there were other things I loved, too. I missed my girls when I was away. Whatever I decided about retirement, I knew I'd already fulfilled my baseball dream, and then some.

Now, reclined on the bus, I drifted back to my meeting with Willie Randolph. "Okay," I told him in his office, friendly but not wholly resigned. "You're the skipper. I'll do whatever you ask of me. A shot at a ring matters to me more than my playing time. But this team is better with me on the field."

"You may be right, Shawn," he said, "but I've got to trust my instincts. Thanks for being such a pro about this."

Yes, I could have objected more vehemently.

But I no longer had the intense drive to show everyone what I could do, to prove them all wrong.

What did this mean? I wondered. Had I already let go, moved on?

When everyone was settled, the bus jerked from park into drive, and we all started moving forward. I stretched out my legs, not uncomfortable with the uncertainty of my situation.

The big leagues on the one hand, more time with my family on the other . . . not easy.

But what a fortunate man I was to have such options in the first place!

• • •

I made my decision about retirement a few weeks later aboard a red-eye flight from Los Angeles to New York, where Lindsay and the girls were living in our summer apartment. Each year, the team took one or two of these coast-to-coast, nighttime jaunts. Our game that night at Dodger Stadium had ended at about nine forty-five and the wheels of the plane were off the ground at LAX by 11:30. That's how quickly teams scramble out of a stadium on getaway day, thanks in large part to everyone's bags being already packed and waiting immediately after the last out. It's all very efficient—the clubhouses are also run by pros.

When I first glanced at my watch aboard the plane it read four forty-five (I hadn't bothered to reset it for the three days we'd been away from the East Coast). We were almost halfway home, thirty-five thousand feet above the heartland of America. I'd just finished an hour-long card game with David Wright, preceded by a couple of chess matches against John Maine. Every team has different games of choice for the flights. When I was with the Blue Jays, we'd played a lot of cards. Sometimes, coaches and other staff members played as well, though we had to kick one coach out of our game for cheating! Then Jose Cruz got Alex Gonzalez, Ed Sprague, and me all fired up on chess. With the Dodgers, I'd played cards with Adrian Beltre, Paul Lo Duca, and Jose Lima, which made for hilarious, nonstop, trash-talking sessions. During my final year in Los Angeles, Texas Hold 'em became popular and half the team played tournament style. It was good for team chemistry. My brief time with the Diamondbacks had been spent flying with some of the most intellectual guys I've played with: Craig Counsell, Andy Green, Shawn Estes, Jose Cruz, and coaches Mike Aldrete and Jay Bell. We got hooked on bridge one year and Scrabble the next. This Mets team had a strong chess contingency, initiated the previous year by catcher Mike DiFelice. I liked just about any game. I didn't care too much about winning, but enjoyed the camaraderie and light-hearted talk. After my friend Darrin Fletcher retired from the Blue Jays a few years before, I asked him what he missed most about baseball. His answer surprised me. Now, it didn't surprise me so much. "I miss the flights," he said.

I'll miss the flights, too, I thought now.

Yes, some people were bound to say it was crazy for me to walk away from the game before my thirty-fifth birthday. I'd made plenty of money, but retirement still meant passing on healthy paychecks. Also, I was only a few home runs behind Hank Greenberg, the all-time Jewish home run leader, and I wasn't likely to catch him with what was left of this season. With the right situation on the right team, I knew I could rediscover my groove and put up big numbers, and such a renewal could put me on a Hall of Fame track. But I couldn't help asking myself: at what cost? Didn't more baseball mean I'd miss that much more of my growing family? In a year, Presley would start kindergarten and, since the day she was born, I'd envisioned being there to walk her into school that first day. In that light, career achievements didn't matter very much.

Most of my teammates were asleep, iPod buds in their ears and blankets covering them as they lay across their three seats. (Everyone but a few rookies got his own row). But one unmistakably large, bald head remained upright, lit from the glow of the computer screen before him. I got up and walked over to my old friend Carlos. He was messing around with pictures of his baby boy on iPhoto. As I stopped at his row, I felt as if I'd gone back twelve or thirteen years to when we were young players for the Blue Jays. In those days, Carlos, Alex Gonzalez, and I were inseparable, the three amigos. We'd come up through the minor leagues together and had entered the big leagues together. Back then, we had to share a row on the plane: The Blue Jay veterans were strict with the young players; these days, the Mets vets took it easier on the kids.

We three amigos had had long careers. Alex had just recently retired. He'd been the first to get married and to have kids, and he was the first to leave the game. I'd been the next to marry and have kids and would be the next to go. Carlos's son was still only a few months old. Besides, Carlos was approaching 500 home runs, a monumental achievement. I hoped he'd get there. Of the three of us, he was the one who could still get into the Hall.

"Flaco, what's going on?" he asked as I sat beside him.

"How many miles do you think we've flown together over the years?" I asked him.

"A lot. Crazy how fast it goes, huh?"

"The flying days are over for me," I told him. "I wanted you to be the first to know. This'll be my last cross-country red-eye with you jokers."

"You've made up your mind?"

"Yes."

"Good for you, Flaco. You've had a great career. I don't blame you for wanting to be home. In a few years, I'll ride off into the Puerto Rican sunset as well. 'Course, I still got a little work to do. Tell me one thing though, how does it feel?"

"What do you mean?"

"How does it feel when you know you're done?"

Carlos had always been like my big brother, and yet here he was asking me a question about his own future. In this way, at least, I was suddenly farther down the line than he was.

"Actually, it feels a lot like when you first put on a big league uniform. You might not think it would. But love brings you into this game as a kid and now, for me, love is taking me out. It's exciting." I didn't have to elaborate on how I felt about Lindsay and the girls—he knew.

"It's been quite a ride for us, eh, Flaco?"

I agreed. Carlos and I had both had stellar seasons and disappointing seasons. We'd gone through countless hot streaks and countless slumps. We'd both struck out four times in games, and we each had had a four home run game (being only the fourteenth and fifteenth players in MLB history to do so). We'd changed teams and leagues, and we'd watched our teammates and friends shuffle in and out of clubhouses overnight. "Lots of ups and downs, comings and goings," I said. "Lots of changes."

He nodded. "That's the way it is, Flaco."

"The way of baseball," I said.

Everything on the surface of life is flux. As a young player, I related only to that superficial level, and so the circumstances of my life dictated my sense of happiness. But as my awareness broadened, I realized that reality runs much deeper.

"The way of baseball . . ." Carlos mused. "That's good, Flaco."

"The way of life."

Carlos grinned. "It looks like my work here is done."

"Mine, too."

"I'm happy for you," he said.

I started to my seat a few rows behind his.

He called back to me with a wry grin. "I don't think I'll be too far behind you, big brother."

Once back in my seat, I looked around the plane. It was strange to feel so fully awake when almost everyone else was fast asleep. Maybe I was growing delirious as the hour neared six in the morning. Or maybe this energetic feeling arose because I had come to a decision to disengage from a path I'd trodden my whole life. Was I feeling the promise of the unknown? I scanned the plane and saw my teammates and good friends, and I realized that the full aliveness I felt was actually no different from what I'd felt five years before on my record-setting day in Milwaukee. It was *presence*, no different from what I'd felt when I first held Lindsay's hand or my newborn daughters.

Life is filled with moments that seem to just pass us by, indeed, moments that we rush through in order to get to other, bigger moments. What a waste! Why isn't every moment treated as sacred and beautiful? Circling the bases or sitting on a red-eye flight . . . what makes one moment more important than another? Maybe life is really just one beautiful moment constantly changing shape. Sure, we sometimes notice the world: crashing waves, a starry night, the majesty of a rainstorm, but we miss most moments. My out of the ordinary public life was about to end. Yet I was excited to embrace the prospect of finding as heightened a state of awareness in my new life as I'd ever known when hitting a ninety-five miles per hour fastball with the sweet spot of my bat.

When we disembarked at JFK, descending the portable stairs that lead to the tarmac, I saw the sun rising over the city where Lindsay and the girls were still sleeping. Before the sun got much higher I'd be home and I'd wake them all for the new day.

EPILOGUE

My game flowered from spiritual roots planted in the dingy underbellies of stadiums even more than on the well-manicured grass under the bright lights. Before I could play with grace and peace in front of fifty thousand people at the old Yankee Stadium, I had to discover stillness deep below the stands in the stadium's batting dungeon, which was located between first base and the right-field foul pole. There, beneath a low ceiling pocked with exposed asbestos, a couple of cages had been thrown together some time after Babe Ruth called this ballpark his office. Other old stadiums, such as Wrigley Field and the old Tiger Stadium, required a hike from the dugout to the outfield wall to even find their cages, which consisted only of musty, rigged-up nets inside the bleachers. Wrigley's cage, which is located in the wall beyond the ivy in right field, isn't even big enough for someone to sit inside and wait for his turn to hit. Instead, visiting players have to stand out on the warning track and listen to the soon-to-be-drunk fans tell them how much they suck. At Fenway Park, the cage is located inside the famous Green Monster in left field, near the grounds crew equipment. Much like the stadium, the cage has a quirky shape to work in an awkward space, but what matters is never so much the place as the attitude and mind-set you bring to it. Fenway's cage was among my favorites. After all, where else can you meditate and find peace inside a monster?

From time to time, we all need to get inside the monster in our lives before we can emerge into the bright lights.

Not long ago I walked into my childhood friend Ben's tiny hitting school, located beside the Newport Freeway in Southern California just a few miles from where I played my high school ball. Accompanied by four nine-year-old Little Leaguers from my daughters' elementary school, I carried my Tanner Tee as a samurai carries his sword (okay, maybe not quite so majestically). The uniformed kids—a Yankee, a Blue Jay, a Brewer, and a Tiger—had won a charity raffle and were to be my students for the day. I greeted Ben, grabbed two big buckets of balls, and led my enthusiastic contingent to the well-worn cage.

After setting up the tee, I turned to my assembly of four. "The first thing you all have to remember is that the game is about one thing," I said.

"Winning?" asked one of the boys.

Too many Under Armour and Gatorade commercials . . . I shook my head *no*. "It's about fun."

"Oh, good," the four kids muttered, relieved to be spared a hard-driving adult.

I tapped the Tanner Tee with my bat. "A tee like this is a very special thing," I said.

The Tiger shrugged. "But we finished with those things back in tee ball."

"Yeah, what's so great about a tee?" the Brewer pressed.

"Well, it's not necessarily the tee itself, but the way you attend to it." I turned and placed a ball on the tee. I took my stance. Then I took a breath. I swung: *crack*, and *whoosh*, into the net. It still felt great, as if no time had passed since my last swing as a pro.

"Wow," a couple of kids said.

I picked up another ball, placed it on the tee, took a breath, and swung: *crack*, and *whoosh* into the net.

The kids liked my swing (some general managers still like it, too, and opportunities have come up to play again, but I'm happy with my life as it is; with new business ventures, speaking engagements, and the writing of this book, there's plenty for now).

"How'd you hit it so hard, Mr. Green?" the Yankee asked me.

"Weight-lifting?" the Blue Jay inquired.

I shook my head *no*. "It starts just by picking up the ball, and *knowing* you're picking it up as you're doing it. See, it's about paying attention to whatever you do. Want to try?"

The kids scrambled into a line to take their cuts.

On the far side of the cage another kid had caught my eye, a cheerful boy of about eleven whom I thought I recognized. Was he a friend's son or maybe a student at the girls' school? No. Was he from the local Little League? No. Then it hit me.

He was the boy I'd seen in my parents' hitting school

back in 2000! Yes, he was the one whose carefree approach to baseball I had envied just before I left for Japan, the Little Leaguer who'd asked for my autograph even as I was thinking I should be asking for his, the boy who wanted to be like me, even as I was desperate to find a way to be more like him. Amazing! I wanted to talk to him.

Then it hit me: That was ten years ago, which meant that the actual boy from my recollection would be a college student by now, unrecognizable to me.

So, who was this?

Maybe a younger brother? Surely, a different boy.

Everything changes.

And yet, in a way, he was the same boy I'd seen ten years ago, in the joyful manner he went about playing the game. Likewise, he was the same boy I had been myself, more than a quarter century before. We are all so different from one another, and yet we are all so much the same. I watched him sort attentively through the rack of bats to find just the right one. One hundred percent focus. I felt confident that whichever bat he chose would work out great for him.

ACKNOWLEDGMENTS

Writers, filmmakers, and even T-shirt manufacturers have depicted baseball as a metaphor for life. There's the rebirth every spring as the season begins, the ending every fall, and the hibernation during the winter months. For me, however, baseball was not a mere metaphor—it was also my passion and livelihood. It brought me pleasure and pain, and it became the vehicle for spiritual growth that arose unexpectedly.

The writing of this book has been an additionally constructive, eye-opening endeavor. The process provided a deepening of the lessons I learned over my baseball career and thus served to reinforce my understanding that life wisdom truly is universal.

My experiences in baseball are what they are because of many people. In the baseball world, I want to thank the players I both competed with and against, my coaches, and the numerous people who filled the diverse roles of the baseball organizations for which I played (everyone from the trainers and clubhouse guys to the front-office personnel). I also want to thank the fans (of both friendly and hostile natures) as well as the media. These two groups attached a sense of importance and urgency to what would otherwise have been just a "meaningless" child's game, providing the necessary environment for my personal growth to occur.

As for the writing of this book, I have to begin with a huge thanks to my very talented coauthor Gordon McAlpine (and to his wife, Julie, and their three sons for "loaning him" to me for so many hours as we put this book together). I couldn't have had a better teammate throughout the process. I would also like to thank our wonderful editor Kerri Kolen and the other people who helped this project come to fruition: Stephanie Carew, Andrea Bobinski, Linda Loewenthal, David Black, Kelly Sonnack, Marysue Rucci, Kate Ankofski, David Rosenthal, and Jonathan Karp.

I also would like to thank my family. My parents, Ira and Judy, and my sister, Lisa, provided me with the unwavering support to fulfill my dreams. My father was my lifelong hitting coach and my mother was my cheerleader. And thanks to all my relatives (including many whom I didn't know), who were always there for me in stadiums throughout the country.

Finally, there are my three girls.

Thank you to my daughters, Presley and Chandler, both for your unconditional love as well as for being a constant reminder to live in the moment. And, last but not least, thank you Lindsay for being my best friend. You not only "get" me more than anyone else, you also "get" life more than anyone I know. I am so grateful to be able to share my life with the three of you.

A NOTE ABOUT THE COVER ART

In Zen, the ensō is a brushed ink circle symbolizing the moment when the mind is empty yet alert, poised for creativity and flow.